EVERYDAY
SUPER FOOD

JAMIE OLIVER

ecco

An Imprint of HarperCollinsPublishers

ALSO BY JAMIE OLIVER

The Naked Chef
The Return of the Naked Chef
Happy Days with the Naked Chef
Jamie's Kitchen
Jamie's Dinners
Jamie's Italy
Cook with Jamie
Jamie at Home
Jamie's Food Revolution
Jamie's America
Jamie Oliver's Food Escapes
Jamie Oliver's Meals in Minutes
Jamie's Great Britain
Jamie's 15-Minute Meals
Save with Jamie
Jamie's Comfort Food

FOOD PHOTOGRAPHY
Jamie Oliver

OTHER PHOTOGRAPHY
Paul Stuart
Freddie Claire

DESIGN
Superfantastic
wearesuperfantastic.com

DEDICATION

This book is dedicated to my amazing food and nutrition teams, all the recipe testers, all the incredible doctors, scientists, and professors, and of course, all the wonderful, old but still amazingly active people, in some of the healthiest places on the planet, who I've met on the epic journey of creating this book.

CONTENTS

HEALTHY & HAPPY

First of all, thank you for picking up this book and welcome to my *Everyday Super Food*. The ultimate promise in these pages is that every recipe choice is a good choice. Quite simply, I wanted to create a super-safe place celebrating delicious, nutritious, achievable meals that will help you cook your way to a healthier, happier, more productive life.

By the time you read this, I will have reached my fortieth birthday. About 18 months ago, nudging ever closer to it, this upcoming milestone made me pause and look at life slightly differently. I'll be honest: it's taken me on a bit of a personal journey as far as my health is concerned. We all have very different lives—mine is particularly peculiar and I love it—but regardless of our individual circumstances, I think most of us want to achieve and support a happy, healthy family at home; be the best we can be at work; maintain good friendships; continue to experience new things; and have lots of laughs along the way. There's certainly no one-size-fits-all answer and getting it wrong sometimes is all part of the journey. But, in order to give yourself the best chance, good personal health needs to be your utmost priority. So, my philosophy in this book is to help you get it right on the food front, most of the time.

If you pick up just a handful of ideas from this book, you'll start thinking differently about food

I want this book to be a gateway to a more understanding and open relationship with food, as something to feed, fuel, fix, and nourish you, but also as medicine. I want to give you knowledge and a better understanding of food and how to put a balanced meal together. I know it's a cliché, but knowledge really is power—that's what I want you to take from this book. I'm not saying you have to eat from it every day, nor for the rest of your life, but I hope it will arm you with the tools to make the right choices, allowing you to duck and dive at your own pace, mixing up these meals with some naughty days and a few treats—I'm not sure a sustainable healthy relationship with food is achievable without them. Personally, I'm using this book Monday to Thursday/Friday, then hitting up *Comfort Food* at the weekend.

My philosophy in this book is to help you get it right on the food front, most of the time

I believe my job with this book was to go out, learn from some of the best health and nutrition experts out there—doctors, scientists, professors—and travel to some of the healthiest places in the world, absorb as much info as possible, then express the most relevant stuff back to you. So that's exactly what I've done, combined with my 30 years of cooking in order to create these yummy recipes, as well as sharing some bite-sized nuggets of super-useful info that will be relevant to you in your everyday life. I've been bartering and bantering with my nutrition team to ensure that the recipes and ideas are exciting, fun, new, and delicious, and that each one embraces the food groups and different ingredients super-rich in nutrients, vitamins, and minerals that work together in a complementary way. Every recipe reflects the balanced plate philosophy and appropriate portion control to ensure you're getting the right amount of food (see page 260). And you really can eat a super-healthy meal and be satisfied—the recipe testers have been surprised at just how generous some of the portions are!

So, no matter which recipe you choose from each chapter—and there's at least 30 breakfasts, 30 lunches, and 30 dinners—it will first and foremost tickle your taste buds and fill you up, but you can also be sure it will fit within a daily structure of calories that will stand you in really good stead (less than 400 calories for breakfast and under 600 each for lunch and dinner, leaving you with plenty spare for snacks and drinks—see page 261).

And you know what, this book won't break the bank either. My team have costed up all the meals, using the supermarkets, as well as local butchers and fishmongers, and on average it's coming out at just $4.00 per portion at 2015 prices. I don't know about you, but for the health investment you're making by cooking from this book, for me, that's a total bargain.

Whether you use the book faithfully for every meal, or dip in and out of it to supplement other meal choices, my hope is that it will deliver on being that solid source you can always rely on. I wanted to show you what good really looks like for breakfast, lunch, and dinner, plus some exciting snack and drink ideas, so you have a real understanding not just of how to balance your plate, but of how to balance your day, week, and month too.

If you pick up just a handful of ideas from this book, you'll start thinking differently about food and the power it has to directly affect you both physically and mentally, inspiring positive changes not only in the way you eat, but hopefully in the eating habits of the people around you as well. Food is there to be appreciated, shared, and enjoyed, and healthy, nourishing food should be colorful, delicious, and, most importantly, fun.

The ultimate promise in these pages is that every recipe choice is a good choice

Rigorous recipe testing has, as usual, been at the heart of the development of this book because I want you to have success at home, every single time. With such a focus on nutrition, the process of writing it has been very different for me. Quite honestly, it's changed the way I work and how I approach putting a plate of food together. The book has become more of a natural diary for me, and this has meant that I've also photographed all the food myself, as the recipes have often taken time to shape and perfect. What you see in these pages is a real reflection of the journey I've been on, and I'm really proud of this book—a lot has gone into it.

Embrace the book, enjoy it, use it as often as you like, cook for your loved ones, but most importantly, I hope it will capture your curiosity and fuel an interest in getting things right when it comes to food, in a way that really works for you. Good luck.

BREAKFAST

Enriching our bodies at breakfast with tasty, nutritious food that'll help us kick off the day in the best way we can is something we should all embrace. I think a lot of us have been brainwashed into believing we only have time to pour milk over cereal, but that's not true! In this game-changer of a chapter you'll find a whole host of super-quick dishes; batches of incredible things you can make up in advance to serve you well each morning, fitting easily into your normal busy routine; as well as simple ideas for lazier mornings and weekend brunches. All the recipes have a nice mix of the food groups and are less than 400 calories per portion. I hope you love them as much as I do.

BAKED EGGS IN POPPED BEANS
CHERRY TOMATOES, RICOTTA ON TOAST

— Mighty cannellini beans are a great source of protein, high in fiber, and contain vitamin C — as well as magnesium, a mineral that helps our muscles to function properly

SERVES 2

8 oz mixed-color ripe
cherry tomatoes

½ a lemon

extra virgin olive oil

4 sprigs of fresh basil

1 x 14-oz can of cannellini beans

1 good pinch of fennel seeds

2 large eggs

2 slices of whole-grain bread
with seeds

2 heaping teaspoons ricotta
cheese

optional: thick balsamic vinegar

optional: hot chili sauce

Halve the tomatoes, place in a bowl, and toss with the lemon juice, 1 tablespoon of oil, and a pinch of sea salt. Pick, tear, and toss in the basil leaves (reserving the smaller ones for garnish), then leave aside to macerate for a few minutes.

Meanwhile, place a large non-stick frying pan on a high heat. Drain the beans and put into the hot pan with the fennel seeds and a pinch of black pepper. Leave for 5 minutes, shaking occasionally—you want them to char and pop open, bursting their skins. Pour the macerated tomatoes into the pan with 6 tablespoons of water, season, then leave to bubble away vigorously for 1 minute. Crack in an egg on each side, then cover with a lid, plate, or aluminum foil, reduce to a medium-low heat, and slow-cook for 3 to 4 minutes for nice soft eggs, or longer if you prefer. Meanwhile, toast the bread.

Divide the ricotta and spread over the two pieces of hot toast, then serve on the side of the baked eggs in beans. Sprinkle the reserved baby basil leaves over the top and tuck right in. Nice finished with a drizzle of balsamic vinegar and/or a drizzle of hot chili sauce. Delicious.

CALORIES	FAT	SAT FAT	PROTEIN	CARBS	SUGAR	FIBER	20 MINUTES
399kcal	15.7g	3.6g	22g	40.7g	5.8g	12.6g	

AWESOME GRANOLA DUST
NUTS, SEEDS, OATS & FRUIT GALORE

Mornings will be amazingly fast and convenient with this epic megamix of brilliant
ingredients, giving us loads of nutritional benefits from the nuts, seeds, oats, and fruit

MAKES 32 PORTIONS

10 cups rolled oats

8 oz raw unsalted mixed nuts,
such as walnuts, Brazils,
hazelnuts, pecans, pistachios,
cashews

3½ oz mixed seeds, such as
chia, poppy, sunflower,
sesame, flaxseed, pumpkin

8 oz unsweetened mixed dried
fruit, such as blueberries,
cranberries, sour cherries,
mango, apricots, figs, sultanas

3 tablespoons quality cocoa
powder

1 tablespoon freshly ground
coffee

1 large orange

Me and my wife get really frustrated about how so many—in fact most—
breakfast cereals are full of added sugar, and nutritionally aren't the best
start to the day. So, with my nutrition team, I developed this delicious
recipe for us all to enjoy—make a big batch and it'll last a couple of weeks
(or more!). Turn the page for loads of fantastic ways we use it—we love it!

Preheat the oven to 350°F. Place the oats, nuts, and seeds in your largest
roasting pan. Toss together and roast for 15 minutes, stirring halfway. Stir the
dried fruit, cocoa, and coffee into the mix, finely grate over the orange zest,
then, in batches, simply blitz to a rough powder in a food processor, tipping
it into a large airtight jar as you go for safekeeping.

To serve, you can have loads of fun—the simplest way is a scant ½ cup of
granola dust per person, either with cold cow's, goat's, soya, nut, or oat milk
or 2 tablespoons of plain yogurt and a handful of fresh fruit (3 oz is one of
our 5-a-day).

You can make porridge by adding a scant ½ **cup of granola dust** to ¾ **cup
of milk**, then top with fresh fruit, and this ratio also works for a smoothie—I
like to chuck **1 ripe banana** and **1 handful of frozen raspberries** into the mix
too. It's even a great base for pancakes—simply beat **2 heaping tablespoons
of granola dust** with **1 heaping tablespoon of whole-grain self-rising flour,
1 mashed banana**, and **1 egg**, then cook as normal. And in winter, try a hot
drink—heat a scant ¼ **cup of granola dust** with ¾ **cup of your favorite milk**
to your desired consistency.

CALORIES	FAT	SAT FAT	PROTEIN	CARBS	SUGAR	FIBER	25 MINUTES
400kcal	14.7g	3.8g	14.7g	52.1g	32.2g	8.2g	

MAGIC POACHED EGG
SMASHED AVO & SEEDED TOAST

— Our brains love protein in the morning, and eggs are a fantastic, affordable source —
that are quick to cook. With a kick of chile, this dish will wake us up and lift our spirits

SERVES 2

olive oil

½–1 fresh red chile

2 large eggs

2 ripe tomatoes

extra virgin olive oil

¼ of a small red onion

1 lime

½ a ripe avocado

2 thick slices of whole-wheat
   bread with seeds

4 sprigs of fresh cilantro

Lay a 12-inch sheet of good-quality plastic wrap flat on a work surface and rub with a little olive oil. Finely slice half the chile (seed if you like) and scatter in the center of the sheet, then carefully crack an egg on top. Pull in the sides of the plastic wrap and, importantly, gently squeeze out any air around the egg. Tie a knot in the plastic wrap to secure the egg snugly inside. Repeat with the remaining chile and the second egg, then put the parcels to one side. Place a pan of water on a medium heat and bring to a simmer.

Use a small, sharp knife to remove the core from the tomatoes, then drop them into the simmering water for just 40 seconds. Remove to cold water, then peel and chop into eighths, discarding the seedy center. Place in a bowl with 1 teaspoon of extra virgin olive oil. Peel and coarsely grate in the onion, mix together, then season to taste with sea salt, black pepper, and half the lime juice. Poach the eggs in the simmering water for around 6 minutes for soft-boiled, or until cooked to your liking.

Meanwhile, peel, pit, and smash up the avo with the remaining lime juice and season to perfection. Toast the bread, then divide and spread the smashed avo on it like butter, and spoon over the dressed tomato. Unwrap your eggs and place them proudly on top, then finish with the cilantro leaves.

CALORIES	FAT	SAT FAT	PROTEIN	CARBS	SUGAR	FIBER	10 MINUTES
258kcal	13.9g	3.2g	12.6g	23g	5.1g	5g	

SMOOTHIE PANCAKES
BERRIES, BANANA, YOGURT & NUTS

— The high-fiber whole-grain flour in these super-pancakes will help keep us full till lunch, plus we get one of our 5-a-day and a nice vitamin C boost from the fruit —

MAKES 4 PORTIONS

11 oz blueberries or raspberries

1 ripe banana

¾ cup reduced-fat (2%) milk

1 large egg

1¾ cups whole-grain self-rising flour

4 tablespoons plain yogurt

ground cinnamon

1 oz chopped raw unsalted mixed nuts, such as walnuts, pecans, hazelnuts

manuka honey

Blitz half the blueberries or raspberries, the peeled banana, milk, egg, and flour in a blender to make a smoothie pancake batter. Tip into a bowl and fold in the remaining berries. Place a large non-stick frying pan on a medium–high heat. Once hot, put your batter into the pan to make large pancakes or little ones, whichever you fancy. Either way, cook for a couple of minutes on each side, or until crisp and golden. Sometimes I flip them for an additional 30 seconds on each brown side to ensure they get super-crispy. Serve as and when they're ready, while you get on with more.

To serve, I like to slice my pancakes in half so you can see all that lovely fruit, like in the picture. Top with a dollop of yogurt, a sprinkling of cinnamon, and a scattering of toasted nuts, then finish with a little drizzle of honey.

> Once you've made the pancake batter, you can cook it right away or pop it into the fridge to keep for up to 3 days, to use each morning.

> If you can't find whole-grain self-rising flour, you can add 2 teaspoons of baking powder per 1 cup of regular whole-wheat flour and sift well.

CALORIES	FAT	SAT FAT	PROTEIN	CARBS	SUGAR	FIBER	20 MINUTES
357kcal	10g	2.2g	13.3g	54.9g	17g	8.9g	

MEXICAN PAN-COOKED BREKKIE
EGGS, BEANS, TOMATOES, MUSHROOMS

— Wonderful little black beans are the highest-protein bean, so are great for brekkie, —
especially if we exercise in the morning as protein helps our muscles to repair

SERVES 2

olive oil

2 ripe mixed-color tomatoes

6 chestnut or cremini
    mushrooms

2 large eggs

½ x 14-oz can of black beans

Worcestershire sauce

1 whole-grain tortilla

2 tablespoons cottage cheese

2 sprigs of fresh cilantro

Tabasco chipotle sauce

Put a 10-inch frying pan on a medium heat with 2 teaspoons of oil. Halve the tomatoes and add cut-side down. Slice the rims and stems off the mushrooms, exposing the whole inside, and place facedown in the pan (keep the trimmings for another day). Cook for 6 to 7 minutes, gently twiddling the tomatoes and mushrooms in the oil and turning only when beautifully golden.

Reduce the heat to low and crack the eggs into the pan, angling it so the whites completely coat the base to create a yummy eggy plate. Working fairly quickly, drain the beans and toss with a splash of Worcestershire sauce, then scatter into the pan. Sprinkle with a pinch of sea salt and black pepper from a height, then cover the pan with a lid, plate, or aluminum foil and leave for about 2 minutes, or until the eggs are cooked to your liking.

Meanwhile, warm the tortilla in a dry pan for just 1 minute, then slice into ½-inch strips for dipping. Serve the breakfast straight from the pan or slide it onto a sharing plate. Add dollops of cottage cheese, pick and sprinkle over the cilantro leaves, and finish with a drizzle of Tabasco chipotle sauce.

CALORIES	FAT	SAT FAT	PROTEIN	CARBS	SUGAR	FIBER	15 MINUTES
324kcal	13.1g	3.7g	20g	25.7g	4.7g	14.1g	

BLACK RICE PUDDING
MANGO, LIME, PASSION FRUIT & COCONUT

— Hazelnut milk contains vitamin B12, helping us to think properly and stay alert, —
while hazelnuts are super-high in vitamin E, protecting our cells against damage

MAKES 4 JARS

1 cup black rice

1 ripe mango

1 lime

1 tablespoon blanched hazelnuts

1 tablespoon coconut flakes

2 ripe bananas

¾ cup + 5 tablespoons hazelnut
milk

1 tablespoon vanilla extract

optional: manuka honey

4 heaping tablespoons plain
yogurt

2 wrinkly passion fruit

Cook the black rice according to the package instructions, overcooking it slightly so it's plump and sticky, then drain and cool. Meanwhile, peel and pit the mango, blitz the flesh in a blender with the lime juice until smooth, and pour into a bowl. Separately, toast the hazelnuts and coconut in a dry frying pan until lightly golden, then bash up in a pestle and mortar.

Peel the bananas and tear into the blender, then blitz with the hazelnut milk, vanilla extract, and two-thirds of the black rice—depending on the sweetness of your bananas, you could also add a teaspoon of honey. Once smooth, stir that back through the rest of the rice—this will give you great texture and color. Divide between four nice jars or bowls. Spoon over the blitzed mango, squeeze half a passion fruit over each one, then delicately spoon over the yogurt and sprinkle with the hazelnuts and coconut.

> I make these on a Sunday night and stack them up in the fridge, ready
> and waiting to be enjoyed with no effort in the days that follow.

CALORIES	FAT	SAT FAT	PROTEIN	CARBS	SUGAR	FIBER	50 MINUTES
277kcal	6.2g	2.5g	6.5g	48.4g	11.4g	5.2g	

FIGGY BANANA BREAD
BLOOD ORANGE & NUT BUTTER

— Full of healthy ingredients, this beautiful bread uses nutrient-packed whole-grain flour, —
nuts, seeds, and good oil, utilizing the natural sweetness of figs, rather than adding sugar

SERVES 12

8 oz dried figs

⅓ cup cold-pressed canola oil

⅔ cup plain yogurt

1 tablespoon vanilla extract

4 ripe bananas

2 large eggs

1 cup whole-grain self-rising flour

1 heaping teaspoon baking
  powder

¾ cup ground almonds

1 tablespoon poppy seeds

½ teaspoon ground turmeric

1 eating apple

1¾ oz whole almonds

Preheat the oven to 350°F. Line a 10-inch ovenproof frying pan or baking pan with a scrunched sheet of wet parchment paper. Place 7 oz of figs in a food processor with the oil, yogurt, vanilla extract, peeled bananas, and eggs, then blitz until smooth. Add the flour, baking powder, ground almonds, poppy seeds, and turmeric and pulse until just combined, but don't overwork the mixture. Coarsely grate and stir in the apple.

Spoon the mixture into the prepared pan and spread out evenly. Tear over the remaining figs, pushing them in slightly, then chop the almonds and scatter over. Bake for 35 to 40 minutes, or until golden, cooked through, and an inserted skewer comes out clean. Transfer to a wire rack to cool a little.

I like to serve each portion with 1 tablespoon of nut butter (see page 242), 1 tablespoon of plain yogurt, and some wedges of blood orange. Store any extra portions in an airtight container, where it will keep for 2 to 3 days.

> If you can't find whole-grain self-rising flour, you can add 2 teaspoons of baking powder per 1 cup of regular whole-wheat flour and sift well—in which case, don't add the additional baking powder listed in the ingredients.

CALORIES	FAT	SAT FAT	PROTEIN	CARBS	SUGAR	FIBER	
250kcal	15.8g	1.7g	7.5g	29g	20.3g	4g	50 MINUTES

SILKEN OMELET
SPINACH, TOMATO, PARMESAN & RYE

___ Rye bread is super-high in fiber, as well as the mineral manganese, which protects ___
the tissue connecting our organs as well as our bones, keeping us strong and healthy

SERVES 1

1 small slice of rye bread

olive oil

2 large eggs

¼ oz Parmesan cheese

1 handful of baby spinach

hot chili sauce

1 beautifully ripe tomato

This omelet cooks really quickly in a hot pan. The heat of the pan is our friend—it prevents the omelet from sticking. At the same time, we don't want to color the omelet—it really takes no time to cook at all. So, pop the rye bread on to toast. Place a 12-inch non-stick frying pan on a high heat with a drizzle of oil, then wipe it around and out with paper towel.

When the pan's hot, beat the eggs in a bowl for 10 seconds, then pour into the pan and swirl around two or three times to cover the base. Evenly grate the cheese over the egg from a height, then turn the heat off. By the time you've done that, the omelet will be cooked. Use a rubber spatula to gently ease it away from the edges and fold it in half—then I like to roll it up a few times, or fold it into quarters or eighths. If folding and rolling causes you any problems, just think badly folded handkerchief and you'll achieve that lovely texture. Pile the spinach onto your toast and top with the omelet and a few drips of chili sauce. Slice the tomato, sprinkle with a little sea salt, and enjoy on the side.

Feel free to add some torn fresh herbs, such as oregano, Italian parsley, or basil, to your eggs too if you fancy, or to use any other good hard cheese.

CALORIES	FAT	SAT FAT	PROTEIN	CARBS	SUGAR	FIBER	10 MINUTES
259kcal	14.8g	4g	19.3g	14.6g	3.5g	2.6g	

PRETTY FRUIT POTS
TRENDY CHIA & NUT MILK

— Chia seeds are pretty cool if you flavor them well. They're really high in protein and fiber, and a source of magnesium, for strong and healthy bones and teeth —

MAKES 10 POTS

4 small bananas (14 oz)

1 teaspoon vanilla extract

2½ cups chilled hazelnut or
   unsweetened almond milk

⅔ cup chia seeds

10 oz frozen fruit, such as mango
   or mixed berries

½ a lime

Peel and tear 3 bananas into a blender. Add the vanilla extract and 1¼ cups of milk, then blitz until smooth. Pour into a pitcher, and stir in half the chia seeds. Divide between ten pots or cups, then pop into the fridge to start setting.

Meanwhile, tip your chosen frozen fruit (it's really nice to ring the changes and mix things up each time you make these) into the blender, peel and tear in the remaining banana, and add the remaining 1¼ cups of milk and the lime juice. Blitz until smooth, then decant into the pitcher and stir through the remaining chia seeds. Divide between your ten pots or cups, pouring it in gently over the back of a spoon so you get a nice line where the two flavors meet. Return to the fridge, and they'll be good to go in a couple of hours.

> These pretty pots are great for up to 3 days after you've made them. Each morning you can top them with any fresh fruit, granola, or toasted nuts you've got, so have fun with it, and enjoy this happy colorful brekkie.

CALORIES	FAT	SAT FAT	PROTEIN	CARBS	SUGAR	FIBER	15 MINUTES PLUS CHILLING
117kcal	4.9g	0.6g	3.2g	14.7g	11.9g	6g	

PROTEIN PORRIDGE
BLENDED OATS, SEEDS, NUTS & QUINOA

— Protein is a macronutrient that helps keep our appetites at bay—this lovely megamix of oats, —
seeds, nuts, and brilliant quinoa will ensure we're getting a lovely morning protein boost

MAKES 14 PORTIONS

4 cups rolled oats

⅔ cup flaxseeds

1¾ oz shelled walnuts

1¾ oz shelled pistachios

1¾ oz whole almonds

¼ cup regular, black, or red
   quinoa

2 teaspoons vanilla extract

3 tablespoons malted powder,
   such as Horlicks or Ovaltine

FOR EACH PORTION

⅔ cup of your favorite milk,
   such as cow's, goat's, soya, nut,
   or oat

3 oz seasonal berries, such
   as blueberries, raspberries,
   blackberries

1 heaping teaspoon chopped raw
   unsalted mixed nuts

> Make up a batch of this protein porridge powder and it'll easily keep for
> a couple of weeks, making mornings a breeze. Just cook up, and enjoy.

In a blender, simply blitz the oats, flaxseeds, and all the nuts, the quinoa, vanilla extract, and malted powder until fine and combined, giving it a shake and working in batches if you need to. Decant the porridge powder into an airtight jar or can, and keep covered, ready to use whenever you like.

When you want a portion, simply place 1¾ oz of protein porridge mixture in a small pan with ⅔ cup of your favorite milk. Stir regularly for 3 minutes on a medium-low heat, or until thickened to your desired consistency.

I like to mash up half my fruit with a fork and stir it through the porridge to give it color, flavor, and natural sweetness, then serve the rest sprinkled on top with the nuts—toast them first if you like, for extra flavor. Yum.

CALORIES	FAT	SAT FAT	PROTEIN	CARBS	SUGAR	FIBER	20 MINUTES
347kcal	17.4g	3.4g	14.4g	32g	13.2g	7.7g	

VEGEREE NOT KEDGEREE
SPICED RICE, VEG, EGGS & YOGURT

Using veg instead of fish starts us off with two of our 5-a-day, plus all the nutrients that
go with them, and the egg provides good protein to help us feel fuller for longer

SERVES 2

¾ cup brown basmati rice

2 large eggs

4 chestnut or cremini
mushrooms

1¼-inch piece of fresh gingerroot

1 fresh red chile

½ a bunch of fresh cilantro
(½ oz)

2 scallions

olive oil

medium curry powder

3½ oz ripe cherry tomatoes

3½ oz frozen peas

3½ oz baby spinach

1 lemon

2 heaping tablespoons fat-free
plain yogurt

Cook the rice in a pan of boiling salted water according to the package instructions, adding the eggs to the pan to soft-boil for the last 6 minutes.

Meanwhile, place a large non-stick frying pan on a medium-high heat. Quarter the mushrooms and place in the dry pan, stirring occasionally, while you peel the ginger and seed the chile. Saving a few slices of chile for garnish, finely chop the rest with the ginger, half the cilantro leaves, and all the stems. Trim and slice the scallions. Push the mushrooms to one side of the pan, then add 1 tablespoon of oil, the chopped ginger, chile, cilantro, and scallions, and 1½ heaping teaspoons of curry powder. Stir-fry for 2 minutes, while you halve and add the tomatoes, followed by the peas and spinach. Drain and add the rice. Toss, stir regularly, and fry for 4 minutes, then squeeze in half the lemon juice and season to perfection.

Briefly hold the eggs under cold running water until cool enough to handle, then peel, halve, and dot in and around the vegeree. Spoon over the yogurt, sprinkle with the reserved chile and cilantro leaves, add an extra pinch of curry powder, and serve right away, with lemon wedges for squeezing over.

CALORIES	FAT	SAT FAT	PROTEIN	CARBS	SUGAR	FIBER	30 MINUTES
400kcal	9.5g	2.2g	16.3g	67.2g	6.8g	5.5g	

FRUIT SOUPS
YOGURT & GRANOLA DUST

___ Think of this as a smoothie in a bowl and you'll absolutely love it. Chia seeds are super-high ___
in fiber, a macronutrient that helps keep us regular and keeps our bowels nice and healthy

ALL SERVE 1

MINT & KIWI

In a blender, blitz **8 fresh mint leaves, 2 peeled kiwi-fruit, 1 handful of baby spinach, 2 heaping table-spoons of chia seeds,** and 1 regular cup of boiling water until smooth, sweetening with a little **liquid honey** if you like. Decant into a bowl, and top with **1 heaping tablespoon of plain yogurt, 1 handful of granola dust** (see page 18), and some **fresh fruit.** Serve straight away or chill, if you prefer.

NETTLE TEA & BLACKBERRY

Make **1 cup of nettle tea.** Once brewed, strain into a blender and blitz with **3½ oz of blackberries** and **2 heaping tablespoons of chia seeds** until smooth, sweetening with a little **liquid honey** if you like. Decant into a bowl, and top with **1 heaping tablespoon of plain yogurt, 1 handful of granola dust** (see page 18), and some **fresh fruit.** Serve straight away or chill, if you prefer.

BASIL & STRAWBERRY

In a blender, blitz **8 fresh basil leaves, 3½ oz of hulled strawberries, 1 teaspoon of balsamic vinegar, 2 heaping tablespoons of chia seeds,** and 1 cup of boiling water until smooth, sweetening with a little **liquid honey** if you like. Decant into a bowl, and top with **1 heaping tablespoon of plain yogurt, 1 handful of granola dust** (see page 18), and some **fresh fruit.** Serve straight away or chill, if you prefer.

GINGER TEA & MANGO

Make **1 cup of ginger tea.** Once brewed, strain into a blender and blitz with **3½ oz of frozen mango, ½ a level teaspoon of ground turmeric, the juice of ½ a lime,** and **2 heaping tablespoons of chia seeds** until smooth, sweetening with a little **liquid honey** if you like. Decant into a bowl, and top with **1 heaping table-spoon of plain yogurt, 1 handful of granola dust** (see page 18), and some **fresh fruit.** Serve straight away or chill, if you prefer.

CALORIES	FAT	SAT FAT	PROTEIN	CARBS	SUGAR	FIBER	5 MINUTES
375kcal	18.1g	2.5g	14.1g	36.1g	23.5g	19.6g	

HARISSA WAFFLES
SESAME FRIED EGGS & CARROT SALAD

___ There's lots of goodness in these waffles—whole-grain flour gives fiber to fill us up and keep ___
pre-lunch hunger pangs at bay, while milk provides an all-important hit of calcium

SERVES 2

¾ cup whole-grain self-rising
   flour

1 tablespoon poppy seeds

2 teaspoons harissa

3 large eggs

6 tablespoons reduced-fat (2%)
   milk

sesame oil

sesame seeds

1 large carrot

1¾ oz baby spinach

1 pomegranate

2 sprigs of fresh mint

2 tablespoons fat-free plain
   yogurt

hot chili sauce

Preheat your waffle iron. In a bowl, mix the flour, poppy seeds, harissa, and 1 egg together, then gradually add the milk, whisking until combined, and season with sea salt and black pepper. Brush the waffle iron with a minimal amount of sesame oil, then sprinkle half a teaspoon of sesame seeds into each side, followed by a quarter of your waffle mixture each side—I make two small waffles, rather than one big one, per person by only part-filling each mold, giving you the ability to make a waffle sandwich later! Cook the waffles for a few minutes, or until golden, fluffy, and cooked through.

Meanwhile, peel and matchstick the carrot, ideally on a mandolin (use the guard!), place in a bowl, then finely slice and add the spinach. Halve the pomegranate, then, holding one half cut-side down in your fingers, bash the back with a spoon so the seeds tumble into the bowl. Squeeze the other half through your fingers so the juice dresses the salad. Toss together, then pick and tear over the mint leaves. Drizzle a small non-stick frying pan on a medium heat with oil, then wipe around and out with paper towel. Crack in 1 of the remaining eggs, sprinkle with a pinch of sesame seeds, then cover the pan to set the top of the egg and cook to your liking.

Serve the waffles with half the salad, the sesame fried egg, a dollop of yogurt, and a good shake of chili sauce, then get on with your second portion.

> If you can't find whole-grain self-rising flour, you can add 2 teaspoons
> of baking powder per 1 cup of regular whole-wheat flour and sift well.

CALORIES	FAT	SAT FAT	PROTEIN	CARBS	SUGAR	FIBER	25 MINUTES
366kcal	15g	3.7g	23g	41.5g	11.4g	8.4g	

RYE SODA BREAD
SUPER-FAST, SUPER-EASY

— Rye flour is high in lots of essential nutrients, especially phosphorus. Adding oats to the equation really ups the fiber content of the loaf too—it's a real all-rounder —

SERVES 6

1¾ cups whole-grain flour, plus extra for dusting

1 cup rye flour

½ cup rolled oats

1 teaspoon baking soda

1 large egg

1¼ cups buttermilk or plain yogurt

This bread is delicious hot from the oven—it requires no proofing in the making, and there are lots of wonderful ways to enjoy it. Preheat the oven to 375°F. Place both flours, the oats, baking soda, and 1 level teaspoon of sea salt in a large bowl and mix together. In a separate bowl, whisk the egg and buttermilk or yogurt together, then use a fork to stir the egg mixture into the flour. Once it starts to come together, use your lightly floured clean hands to pat and bring the dough together.

Shape the dough into a round ball and place on a lightly floured baking sheet, dusting the top lightly with flour too. Use your hands to flatten the dough into a disk, roughly 1¼ inches deep. Score a cross or star into the top with a knife, about ¼ inch deep, then bake in the center of the oven for 40 to 45 minutes, or until a firm crust has formed and it sounds hollow when tapped on the bottom.

Transfer to a wire cooling rack, and serve slightly warm. As you'd expect, this is great with all your favorite toppings. For lots of ideas, see page 70.

CALORIES	FAT	SAT FAT	PROTEIN	CARBS	SUGAR	FIBER	50 MINUTES
248kcal	3.3g	0.7g	10.4g	46.5g	3.5g	6.5g	

PERFECT PORRIDGE OAT BARS
NUTS, SEEDS, FRUIT & SPICES

___ These portable bars are packed with lots of complementary nutritious ingredients, such ___
as iron-rich dried apricots, which the vitamin C in the orange helps us to absorb

MAKES 12 PORTIONS

3½ oz unsalted mixed nuts, such
as walnuts, Brazils, hazelnuts,
pecans, pistachios, cashews

1¾ oz mixed seeds, such as chia,
poppy, sunflower, sesame,
flaxseed, pumpkin

3½ oz mixed dried fruit, such as
blueberries, cranberries, sour
cherries, mango, apricots, figs,
sultanas

1 heaping teaspoon ground
ginger

½ teaspoon ground turmeric

1 orange

2 ripe bananas

1 tablespoon liquid honey

1¾ cups rolled oats

1 tablespoon oat bran

Preheat the oven to 375°F. In a food processor, pulse the nuts, seeds, dried fruit, and spices with the finely grated orange zest, then tip into a bowl. Peel the orange, then blitz the segments to a pulp with the peeled bananas in the processor. Pour the mixture into a measuring cup, add the honey, and top up to 2 cups total volume with water. Pour into a large pan on a medium-high heat and just bring to a boil, then use a rubber spatula to stir in the oats, bran, and blitzed nut mixture. Keep stirring, beating, and mashing over the heat for 5 minutes, or until the oats start releasing their starch and the mixture becomes gluey.

Transfer to a non-stick 10-inch square baking pan. Spread it out and, to help you later, score your twelve bar portions into the top. Bake at the bottom of the oven for 45 to 50 minutes, or until golden and set. Leave to cool in the pan for 10 minutes, then transfer to a wire rack.

> Store your porridge oat bars in an airtight container in the fridge for up to 3 days. For a balanced brekkie, enjoy with fresh fruit and a glass of milk.

CALORIES	FAT	SAT FAT	PROTEIN	CARBS	SUGAR	FIBER	1 HOUR
171kcal	9g	1.2g	4.4g	20.8g	11.6g	3.6g	

BREAKFAST POPOVERS
CHEESE, HAM, MUSHROOM & TOMATO

— As well as being super-quick and tasty, cottage cheese, eggs, and ham all give us satiating —
protein, helping our muscles to repair and recover and helping to keep us full till lunch

SERVES 2

1 heaping tablespoon whole-grain
self-rising flour

1 large egg

2 heaping tablespoons cottage
cheese

1 slice of quality smoked ham

1 ripe plum tomato

2 chestnut or cremini mushrooms

½ oz Parmesan cheese

hot chili sauce

2 tablespoons plain yogurt

2 handfuls of arugula

½ a lemon

Place the flour in a bowl and beat well with the egg and cottage cheese. Finely chop the ham, tomato, and mushrooms, and stir through the mixture with a good pinch of sea salt and black pepper. Put a large non-stick frying pan on a medium-low heat. Once hot, put heaping spoonfuls of the mixture into the pan to give you six popovers. Leave them to get nicely golden for a few minutes, then flip over and gently flatten to ½ inch thick with a palette knife.

Once golden on both sides, remove the popovers from the pan for a moment, then turn the heat off. Finely grate the Parmesan into the pan to melt. Place the popovers on top, wait for the Parmesan to sizzle and go golden from the residual heat of the pan, then use your palette knife to gently push the cheese towards each popover. Once the crispy popovers can be easily pried away from the pan with your palette knife, bang them out onto a board.

Swirl some chili sauce through the yogurt, toss the arugula in a squeeze of lemon juice, and serve both on the side, then enjoy!

> If you can't find whole-grain self-rising flour, you can add 2 teaspoons of baking powder per 1 cup of regular whole-wheat flour and sift well.

CALORIES	FAT	SAT FAT	PROTEIN	CARBS	SUGAR	FIBER	
189kcal	9g	4g	15.1g	11.8g	4.3g	2.5g	10 MINUTES

BERRY POCKET EGGY BREAD
PISTACHIOS, YOGURT, HONEY & CINNAMON

— Crunchy pistachios are super-high in the mineral chloride, which our bodies need to make hydrochloric acid in the stomach, in turn aiding good digestion and keeping our gut happy —

SERVES 2

2 large eggs

1 small ripe banana

ground nutmeg

ground cinnamon

2 thick slices of whole-grain bread with seeds

5 oz raspberries

olive oil

¾ oz shelled pistachios

4 heaping tablespoons fat-free plain yogurt

manuka honey

In a blender, blitz the eggs, peeled banana, and 1 pinch each of nutmeg and cinnamon until smooth, then pour into a wide shallow bowl. Cut your bread 1 inch thick, then cut a slit into the longest side of each slice and wiggle your knife inside to make a pocket. Use your finger to stuff the raspberries inside—pack as many in as you can, but be gentle so you don't tear the bread. Lay in the eggy mixture and gently squash the bread so it soaks up the eggs.

Meanwhile, put a large non-stick frying pan on a medium-low heat with 1 teaspoon of oil, then wipe it around and out with paper towel. Pour half the excess egg mixture into one side of the pan, then place a piece of soaked bread on top to give it a lovely pancake layer. Repeat with the rest of the mixture and the other slice alongside it. Cook for 3 to 4 minutes, or until golden, then confidently flip over to cook for the same amount of time. Meanwhile, smash up the pistachios in a pestle and mortar—toast them first if you like.

Serve the eggy bread dolloped with yogurt, sprinkled with pistachios and an extra pinch of cinnamon, and drizzled with a little honey.

CALORIES	FAT	SAT FAT	PROTEIN	CARBS	SUGAR	FIBER	15 MINUTES
344kcal	14.4g	3.1g	18.8g	38.2g	17.4g	6.7g	

RAINBOW OPEN WRAP
SALAD, FETA & SPICED CRISPY BEANS

— Packed with a massive four of our 5-a-day, this also heroes black-eyed beans, which are full
of protein, iron, and B vitamins, especially folic acid, important for any expectant mothers —

SERVES 2

½ x 14-oz can of black-eyed beans

sweet smoked paprika

4 heaping tablespoons plain
   yogurt

½ a bunch of fresh cilantro (½ oz)

2 limes

¼ of a small English cucumber

1 small carrot

¼ of a small red cabbage (5 oz)

1 ripe tomato

¼ of an iceberg lettuce

1 fresh red chile

2 spelt or whole-wheat flatbreads

¾ oz feta cheese

Drain the beans well, toss with a good pinch of paprika, tip them into a large non-stick frying pan on a high heat, and simply leave to crisp up for around 10 minutes, or until they crackle and pop, then remove to a plate.

Meanwhile, in a blender, blitz up the yogurt, half the cilantro leaves and all the stems, and the juice of 1 lime to make a simple, clean dressing, then taste and season to perfection. Run your fork lengthwise down the cucumber to create grooves, then finely slice along with the carrot, cabbage, tomato, iceberg, and chile (seed if you like), either by hand with good knife skills, or ideally, for really beautiful results, on a mandolin (use the guard!).

Just warm the flatbreads in the empty frying pan for 20 seconds to make them flexible, then divide the veg between them and top with the crispy beans, a good drizzle of the dressing, and a crumbling of feta. Pick over the remaining cilantro leaves and add an extra squeeze of lime juice if you like, to taste. Roll them up and tuck in—they're a messy eat, but totally delicious. And as great as these are on their own, they're equally brilliant with a little leftover grilled or roasted meat thrown into the mix.

CALORIES	FAT	SAT FAT	PROTEIN	CARBS	SUGAR	FIBER	15 MINUTES
313kcal	8.9g	3g	15.9g	37.2g	10.8g	16.5g	

SCRAMBLED EGGS—PART ONE

Eggs are amazing—just two eggs give us over a day's worth of vitamin B12, which helps our bodies to produce red blood cells, keeping us awake and alert, perfect for the morning

BOTH SERVE 1

SMOKED SALMON & SCALLION EGGS

Pop **1 small slice of sourdough bread** on to toast. Trim **1 scallion** and finely slice it with **1 oz of smoked salmon**. Beat **2 large eggs** with 1 pinch of black pepper, then fold through the sliced scallion and smoked salmon. Put a small non-stick frying pan on a medium heat and wipe with a piece of oiled paper towel. Pour the egg mixture into the pan, and stir every 10 seconds with a rubber spatula until you've got beautiful silky strips of cooked egg, surrounded by softer, custardy egg. Serve on the toast, with **1 wedge of lemon** for squeezing over.

CALORIES	FAT	SAT FAT	PROTEIN	CARBS	SUGAR	FIBER	5 TO 10 MINUTES
315kcal	15g	3.9g	25.1g	20.8g	2.2g	1.3g	

SPINACH, PARMESAN & CHILE EGGS

Pop **1 small slice of whole-grain bread with seeds** on to toast. Put a small non-stick frying pan on a medium heat and wipe with a piece of oiled paper towel. Finely chop **1 handful of baby spinach** and add to the pan to wilt, while you beat **2 large eggs** with 1 small pinch of sea salt and black pepper. Pour the eggs into the pan, finely grate in ¼ **oz of Parmesan cheese**, and stir every 10 seconds with a rubber spatula until you've got beautiful silky strips of cooked egg, surrounded by softer, custardy egg. Serve on the toast, with some sliced **fresh red chile** on top.

CALORIES	FAT	SAT FAT	PROTEIN	CARBS	SUGAR	FIBER	5 TO 10 MINUTES
300kcal	15.2g	4g	22.6g	17.6g	3.1g	3.2g	

SCRAMBLED EGGS—PART TWO

As well as B12, eggs provide a source of nearly all the other B vitamins, plus vitamin D, phosphorus, iodine, selenium, and protein—what a nutritional powerhouse!

BOTH SERVE 1

TOMATO, CHEESE & BASIL EGGS

Pop **1 small slice of rye bread** on to toast. Put a small non-stick frying pan on a medium heat and wipe with a piece of oiled paper towel. Chop **2 ripe tomatoes**, then add to the pan with 1 small pinch of sea salt and black pepper and cook for 5 minutes. Beat **2 large eggs** in a bowl and tear in **8 fresh basil leaves**. Push the thick tomato sauce aside and melt a **¼ oz slice of cheese** on top. Pour the eggs into the pan and stir every 10 seconds with a rubber spatula until you've got beautiful silky strips of cooked egg, surrounded by softer, custardy egg. Fold through the cheesy tomatoes and serve on the toast.

CALORIES	FAT	SAT FAT	PROTEIN	CARBS	SUGAR	FIBER	5 TO 10 MINUTES
270kcal	13.3g	4g	21.3g	18.1g	6.3g	3.4g	

MUSHROOM & MARMITE EGGS

Pop **1 small slice of whole-grain bread with seeds** on to toast. Put a small non-stick frying pan on a medium heat and wipe with a piece of oiled paper towel. Slice **1 handful of button mushrooms**, then add to the pan with **1 teaspoon of Marmite** and a splash of water. Cook for a few minutes while you beat **2 large eggs** with 1 pinch of black pepper. Pour the eggs into the pan and stir every 10 seconds with a rubber spatula until you've got beautiful silky strips of cooked egg, surrounded by softer, custardy egg. Serve on the toast, sprinkled with **1 pinch of cayenne pepper**.

CALORIES	FAT	SAT FAT	PROTEIN	CARBS	SUGAR	FIBER	5 TO 10 MINUTES
265kcal	12.3g	3.3g	22.4g	18.2g	1.7g	3.7g	

QUICK HOMEMADE TORTILLA
SCALDED VEG, CHILI, CHEESE & AVO

— Making quick, delicious wraps like this using whole-grain flour is super-easy and
provides us with a great source of fiber to keep those mid-morning hunger pangs at bay —

SERVES 2

extra virgin olive oil

white wine vinegar

6 spears of asparagus

6 spears of broccolini

2 ripe tomatoes

½ a ripe avocado

1 lime

½ cup whole-grain self-rising
    flour, plus extra for dusting

2 heaping tablespoons cottage
    cheese

hot chili sauce

Mix 1 teaspoon each of oil and vinegar with a pinch of sea salt and black pepper in a large bowl. Put a large frying pan on a high heat. Rinse the asparagus and broccolini, then trim off the tougher ends and split the spears lengthwise (other seasonal greens are great too, so embrace the best that the season has to offer). Place in the hot pan—the moisture from rinsing them will briefly steam the veg before they start to scald and char—turn halfway. Halve the tomatoes across the middle and add to the pan cut-side down. Leave it all for 5 minutes, or until gnarly and on the edge of catching, removing and tossing in the bowl of dressing as and when they're done.

Peel and pit the avocado, smash up in a pestle and mortar until smooth, then muddle in the lime juice and season to perfection. To make your tortillas, simply mix the flour with 3 tablespoons + 1 teaspoon of water and a pinch of salt until you have a smooth, pliable dough. On a lightly floured surface, roll out one half until ⅛ inch thick and about 8 inches in diameter, then cook through and char on one side only in a hot frying pan, so the top bubbles up, and repeat when done. I like to rest them over a rolling pin to give a natural curve to hold your filling.

Serve each tortilla loaded up with scalded veg. Spoon over the smashed avo and cottage cheese, and finish with a drizzle of chili sauce.

> If you can't find whole-grain self-rising flour, you can add 2 teaspoons of baking powder per 1 cup of regular whole-wheat flour and sift well.

CALORIES	FAT	SAT FAT	PROTEIN	CARBS	SUGAR	FIBER	20 MINUTES
235kcal	8.4g	1.7g	10.2g	31.4g	6g	7.4g	

TOASTED OATS
MANGO, BLUEBERRIES & YOGURT

Oats fill us up and act as a slow-burning fuel, so are a perfect start to the day. They're high in fiber, and the minerals phosphorus and magnesium, keeping our bones strong and healthy

SERVES 1

1 handful of rolled oats (1¾ oz)

1 level teaspoon fennel seeds

1 heaping teaspoon coconut flakes

2 heaping tablespoons plain yogurt

1 small handful of blueberries

optional: rose water

1 small ripe mango

½ a banana

½ a lime

optional: manuka honey

Put the oats into a small frying pan on a medium heat with the fennel seeds and coconut and toast until lightly golden and smelling delicious, tossing regularly. Tip into your bowl and spoon the yogurt on top.

Return the pan to the heat. Place the blueberries in with a good splash of water and a few drips of rose water (if using), which will add an incredible perfumed flavor. Simply boil for a couple of minutes until the berries burst and you have a loose sauce, then spoon over the yogurt.

Slice one of the cheeks off the mango and cut a criss-cross pattern into the flesh, making sure you don't go all the way through, then turn it inside out so all the pieces pop up into a mango hedgehog (keep the rest of the mango for another day). Peel and slice the banana, then dress both mango and banana with a squeeze of lime juice. Add to your bowl and tuck right in. Great as it is, or if you like you can drizzle 1 teaspoon of honey over the top before serving.

CALORIES	FAT	SAT FAT	PROTEIN	CARBS	SUGAR	FIBER	10 MINUTES
329kcal	8.3g	3.4g	9.1g	53.5g	19.7g	8.5g	

SWEET POTATO MUFFINS
CHILE, CHEESE & SEEDS

Super sweet potatoes give us vitamin C, helping to protect our cells from damage caused by stress. The eggs, cheese, and seeds also give protein, to help keep us feeling full till lunch

MAKES 6 PORTIONS

olive oil

1¼ lbs sweet potatoes or ½ a butternut squash

4 scallions

1–2 fresh red chiles

6 large eggs

3 tablespoons cottage cheese

1¾ cups whole-grain self-rising flour

1¾ oz Parmesan cheese

1 tablespoon raw sunflower seeds

1 tablespoon poppy seeds

Preheat the oven to 350°F. Line a 12-cup muffin pan with paper liners or 6-inch folded squares of parchment paper, then lightly wipe each one with oiled paper towel. Peel the sweet potatoes or squash and coarsely grate into a large bowl. Trim the scallions, then finely slice with the chile and add to the bowl, reserving half the chile to one side. Crack in the eggs, add the cottage cheese and flour, then finely grate in most of the Parmesan and season with sea salt and black pepper. Mix until nicely combined.

Evenly divide the muffin mixture between the liners. Sprinkle over the sunflower and poppy seeds, then dot over the reserved slices of chile. Use the remaining Parmesan to give a light dusting of cheese over each one, then bake on the bottom rack of the oven for 45 to 50 minutes (if using squash, it'll be a bit quicker—check after 35 minutes), or until golden and set.

These are amazing served warm 5 minutes after taking them out of the oven, and good kept in the fridge for a couple of days. Enjoy 2 muffins per portion.

> I like to make the muffin mixture and divide it up the night before, ready to bake fresh in the morning—that way you can even bake off portions as and when you want to eat them.

> If you can't find whole-grain self-rising flour, you can add 2 teaspoons of baking powder per 1 cup of regular whole-wheat flour and sift well.

CALORIES	FAT	SAT FAT	PROTEIN	CARBS	SUGAR	FIBER	1 HOUR
366kcal	12.5g	3.9g	18.2g	49.2g	7.1g	6.5g	

EPIC FRUIT SALAD
DELICIOUS NATURAL JUICES

I've used a little extra virgin olive oil here so that our body absorbs all of the essential fat-soluble vitamins, such as vitamin E, found in these fruits, plus we get two of our 5-a-day

MAKES 10 PORTIONS

2 wrinkly passion fruit

2 clementines

2 limes

½ a bunch of fresh mint (½ oz)

1 tablespoon cold-pressed extra virgin olive oil

1 teaspoon balsamic vinegar

1 ripe pineapple

1 ripe mango

2 ripe peaches

8 oz strawberries

7 oz blueberries

5 oz blackberries

> Make a big batch of this delicious fruit salad to keep in the fridge and see you through a few days. This is an easy way to eat the good stuff.

Get yourself a big bowl that will fit happily in the fridge. Halve the passion fruit, then spoon the juicy centers into the bowl and squeeze in all the citrus juice. Pick and finely slice the mint leaves, add along with the oil and balsamic vinegar (trust me), and mix together. This will give extra flavor to your fruits, and the acid will stop any discoloring, but feel free to have fun and mix things up by adding flavors such as ginger, lemongrass, fresh basil, lemon balm, vanilla, canned lychees, or even prunes to accent the juices brilliantly.

Now for your fruit—quite simply just prep and cut it all up into random bite-sized pieces that are a pleasure to eat. Avoid using any bruised fruit—that's best frozen for use in smoothies. Add the fruit to the bowl as you prep it, then simply toss it all in the juices, cover, and keep in the fridge until needed.

The combo listed here is one of my favorites, but other great fruit that's resilient enough to hold up includes grapes, melon (but not watermelon), pears, plums, and papaya. Garnish-friendly fruit tends to be softer, such as bananas, raspberries and soft berries, watermelon, and kiwifruit—feel free to add this each time you take a serving to boost your fruit intake further, and remember, eating the rainbow is a wonderful thing. Serve with yogurt or cottage cheese, and toasted nuts and seeds or granola dust (see page 18).

CALORIES	FAT	SAT FAT	PROTEIN	CARBS	SUGAR	FIBER	20 MINUTES
73kcal	1.5g	0.2g	1.1g	14.3g	13.3g	2.5g	

SUPER-FOOD PROTEIN LOAF
WHEAT-FREE, GLUTEN-FREE & TASTY

— For all you morning gym-goers, this healthy protein bread is a great portable breakfast that —
will help with muscle repair and growth—for yummy topping ideas simply turn the page

MAKES 14 PORTIONS

1 x ¼-oz package of dried yeast

4 tablespoons extra virgin
   olive oil

1 cup chickpea flour

¾ cup ground almonds

¼ cup flaxseeds

3½ oz mixed seeds, such as
   chia, poppy, sunflower,
   sesame, pumpkin

1 sprig of fresh rosemary

4 large eggs

optional: 3 teaspoons Marmite

Preheat the oven to 375°F. Line a 6-cup loaf pan with parchment paper. Fill a pitcher with 1½ cups of lukewarm water, add the yeast and oil, then mix with a fork until combined and leave aside for 5 minutes.

Pile the flour, ground almonds, and all the seeds into a large bowl with a pinch of sea salt and make a well in the middle. Pick, finely chop, and add the rosemary leaves. Crack in the eggs, add the Marmite (if using—simply leave it out for a gluten-free friendly loaf), and beat together, then pour in the yeast mixture. Whisking as you go, gradually bring in the flour from the outside until combined—it'll be more like a batter than a dough. Pour into the prepared pan and smooth out nice and evenly on top.

Now you've got two choices—bake it straight away and it'll puff up a bit more and taste fantastic, or cover and place it in the fridge overnight and allow some slightly more complex sour flavors to develop. Both are brilliant, just different. To bake, place in the middle of the oven for 45 minutes, or until golden, cooked through, and an inserted skewer comes out clean. Transfer to a wire rack to cool for at least 20 minutes before eating, then serve.

> This bread is good fresh for a couple of days, and delicious toasted for a few days after that. You could even use any leftovers to make croutons.

CALORIES	FAT	SAT FAT	PROTEIN	CARBS	SUGAR	FIBER	1 HOUR PLUS COOLING
213kcal	14.5g	2g	10g	10.2g	0.9g	5.1g	

SUPER-FOOD PROTEIN LOAF
TOPPING IDEAS GALORE

— This page is all about giving you loads of colorful inspiration for tasty topping combos that'll fill you with goodness—choose your favorites and tuck in —

1. Chopped hard-boiled egg, yogurt, paprika & cress

2. Ripe beef tomatoes, Swiss cheese & black pepper

3. Light cream cheese, ripe cherry tomatoes & fresh basil

4. Cottage cheese, soft-boiled egg, paprika & scallions

5. Wilted spinach & cottage cheese

6. Squashed beet, plain yogurt & balsamic

7. Grated cucumber & cottage cheese with smoked salmon

8. Light cream cheese, cherries & cinnamon

9. Light cream cheese, cucumber & hot chili sauce

10. Light cream cheese, lemony grilled asparagus, fresh mint & chile

11. Plain yogurt, banana & cinnamon

12. Fried egg, plain yogurt, ripe cherry tomatoes & curry powder

13. Avocado, cottage cheese & Tabasco chipotle sauce

14. Hummus, pomegranate seeds & arugula

15. Marmite, ripe avocado & plain yogurt

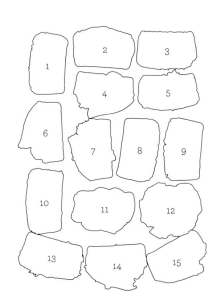

POST-GYM SUPER SALAD
CHICKEN, QUINOA & LOADSA VEG

— Lean chicken and quinoa are excellent protein sources post-exercise, when protein promotes —
muscle growth by repairing damage—for optimal benefit eat within 50 minutes of exercising

SERVES 1

⅓ cup regular, black, or red
  quinoa

¼ of a small English cucumber

¼ of a small iceberg lettuce

½ a small carrot

½ an eating apple

1 ripe tomato

½–1 fresh red chile

2 sprigs of fresh mint

1 small handful of baby spinach

1 lime

1 heaping tablespoon plain
  yogurt

1 teaspoon hot chili sauce

3 oz leftover cooked skinless
  chicken breast

½ cup sprouting cress

Cook the quinoa according to the package instructions, then drain (if you have the opportunity to cook up a batch of quinoa in advance to keep in the fridge ready for this dish, it will save time here).

Get yourself a large chopping board and roughly chop the cucumber, lettuce, carrot, apple, and tomato. Finely chop the chile (seed if you like), pick over the mint leaves, and add the spinach to the story. Squeeze over the lime juice and spoon over the yogurt. Drizzle over the chili sauce, then chop and mix everything together until nice and fine, so all the flavors combine.

Mix in the quinoa, shred up and add the chicken, then have a taste and season to perfection with sea salt, black pepper, and a little more chile or lime juice if you think it needs it. Serve in a bowl, or even a wrap if you're on the go, with the cress sprinkled on the top—delicious.

CALORIES	FAT	SAT FAT	PROTEIN	CARBS	SUGAR	FIBER	30 MINUTES
400kcal	6.8g	1.5g	38.1g	49.6g	19.3g	4.3g	

HEALTHY CHEESE & CORN PANCAKES
SMOKY BACON & CARAMELIZED BANANA

Cottage cheese is a great twist to this batter, making the pancakes super-light and fluffy, and as well as being lower in fat than all other cheeses, it's also super-high in protein

SERVES 4

1 x 12-oz can of sweet corn

6 scallions

1 fresh red chile

2 large eggs

7 oz cottage cheese

1 cup whole-grain self-rising flour

3 tablespoons + 1 teaspoon
   reduced-fat (2%) milk

olive oil

4 slices of smoked bacon

4 small bananas

optional: Tabasco jalapeño sauce

Tip the sweet corn into a bowl, juice and all. Trim the scallions and finely slice with the chile (seed if you like), then add to the bowl along with the eggs, cottage cheese, and flour. Mix together, then gradually loosen with the milk to a thick but oozy batter. Lightly season with sea salt and black pepper.

I like to cook and serve 2 pancakes at a time so each person gets a lovely hot plate of food. Put a large non-stick frying pan on a medium heat and wipe with a piece of oiled paper towel. Place 1 slice of bacon in the pan and as soon as it starts to release its smoky fat, wiggle that around the pan. Add 2 small ladles of batter to one side and flatten them slightly. Peel 1 banana and cut into four chunky slices at an angle. Add them to the pan to caramelize, turning when golden. Once the pancakes are golden on the bottom, flip them over to cook on the other side. Finessing your temperature control so that everything is ready at the same time is an art—just tweak the temperature to help you out until you get your groove.

Get your first lucky customer seated at the table and serve their pancakes with the banana, bacon, and Tabasco (I'm loving the green jalapeño one here) for drizzling, if they fancy it, while you crack on with the next portion.

> If you can't find whole-grain self-rising flour, you can add 2 teaspoons of baking powder per 1 cup of regular whole-wheat flour and sift well.

CALORIES	FAT	SAT FAT	PROTEIN	CARBS	SUGAR	FIBER	30 MINUTES
400kcal	10.7g	4g	18.2g	59.9g	23.8g	6.6g	

SEXY STEWED PRUNES
TOAST, BANANA, YOGURT, ALMONDS

__ Prunes are a fantastic source of fiber, hence their reputation for keeping us regular! __
Paired with yogurt, this brekkie will also help keep our gut bacteria healthy

MAKES 6 PORTIONS

3½ cups prunes in natural juice

2 Earl Grey teabags

1 pinch of ground cloves

¾-inch piece of fresh gingerroot

FOR EACH PORTION

1 thick slice of whole-grain bread
   with seeds

1 tablespoon flaked almonds

½ a banana

1 heaping tablespoon Greek
   yogurt

Drain the prune juice into a pan. Add the teabags and cloves, then peel, finely chop, and add the ginger. Place over a medium heat to bubble and thicken for 7 minutes, while you squeeze the pits out of the prunes. When the time's up, remove and discard the teabags and stir the prunes into the sticky syrup.

For each portion, I pop a slice of bread on to toast while I lightly toast the almonds in a dry frying pan on a medium heat. Slice up the banana and smash it onto your toast with a fork. Spoon over the yogurt, add 1 heaping tablespoon of hot or cold stewed prunes, scatter over the almonds, and devour.

What I love about these delicious, easy stewed prunes is that you can simply make and serve them warm for a crowd, or you can make a batch at the weekend to enjoy throughout the week. They're good kept in the fridge for up to 1 week.

CALORIES	FAT	SAT FAT	PROTEIN	CARBS	SUGAR	FIBER	20 MINUTES
362kcal	9.3g	2.2g	12g	61.2g	40.1g	7.2g	

MY BIRCHER MUESLI
FRUIT, NUTS, YOGURT & SEEDS

— This recipe is full of goodness. It's super-high in fiber, and contains one portion of our 5-a-day plus a super sprinkling of nuts and seeds—a perfect portable start to the day —

MAKES 10 PORTIONS

3½ oz dried apricots

4 cups cow's or nut milk

2 ripe bananas

1 orange

1 fresh bay leaf

1 vanilla bean

5 cups rolled oats

FOR EACH PORTION

2 tablespoons plain yogurt

½ an eating apple or pear

1 teaspoon raw unsalted mixed
  nuts

1 teaspoon mixed seeds

1 handful of seasonal berries

Place the dried apricots in a blender. Pour in the milk, then peel and tear in the bananas. Finely grate in the orange zest, then squeeze in all the juice. Remove the stem from the bay and finely chop the leaf. Halve the vanilla bean lengthwise and scrape out the seeds, then add them to the blender with the bay (pop the vanilla bean in a pot of honey to infuse it with extra flavor, for other meals). Blitz for a few minutes, until super-smooth, then in a bowl mix with the oats and pop into the fridge for at least 2 hours, preferably overnight.

For each portion, add the yogurt and grate over the apple or pear, mixing it through if you like. Toast your nuts and seeds—I like to mix it up each time; try pistachios, cashews, almonds, chia, poppy, sunflower, or flaxseeds—crush and scatter over, then serve with fresh berries.

> This will keep in the fridge for a good 2 days and is a perfect portable breakfast—simply add the toppings each morning and you're away.

CALORIES	FAT	SAT FAT	PROTEIN	CARBS	SUGAR	FIBER	5 MINUTES
358kcal	10.6g	2.4g	10.4g	53.2g	23.7g	8.9g	PLUS SOAKING

PAN-COOKED MUSHROOMS
TOMATO, PANCETTA, SPINACH & CHEESE

— This lovely balanced breakfast heroes the humble mushroom, which is a great source of
copper, one of the essential nutrients our nervous system needs to function efficiently —

SERVES 1

6 chestnut or cremini
   mushrooms

1 ripe tomato

olive oil

white wine vinegar

Tabasco chipotle sauce

1 slice of whole-grain bread with
   seeds

1 slice of smoked pancetta

1 handful of baby spinach

1 tablespoon cottage cheese

Trim off the rims and stems of the mushrooms and place the mushrooms in a bowl (keeping the trimmings for another day). Halve the tomato through the stem, add to the bowl with 1 teaspoon each of oil and vinegar and a few dashes of Tabasco, then toss together. Place a large non-stick frying pan on a medium heat and put the tomato and mushrooms into the pan cut-side down along with the slice of bread and the pancetta.

I like to let everything cook and color for 10 to 15 minutes, turning the tomato and bread halfway. Keep an eye on the pancetta and move it on top of the bread once crispy. Let the mushrooms get really golden on their underside before flipping them. For the last couple of minutes, shake all the ingredients to one side and add the spinach to wilt down. Season to perfection.

Place the toast on your plate, pile the spinach on top, followed by the cottage cheese, tomato, and pancetta. Serve with an extra dash of Tabasco, with those lovely golden mushrooms on the side, season to taste, and tuck straight in.

CALORIES	FAT	SAT FAT	PROTEIN	CARBS	SUGAR	FIBER	
247kcal	11.8g	2.8g	10.4g	23.3g	5.9g	4.6g	20 TO 25 MINUTES

EARL GREY BANANA BREAD
GRIDDLED PEACHES, YOGURT & NUTS

— Potassium-packed bananas keep our nervous system in good shape, assisting our internal body communication and helping us to maintain healthy blood pressure —

SERVES 8

1 Earl Grey teabag

1¾ oz unsweetened dried banana

1¾ oz dried dates

1¾ oz pecans

1 cup whole-grain self-rising flour

½ cup rye flour

1 level teaspoon baking powder

2 large ripe bananas

2 large eggs

3 tablespoons maple syrup

4 tablespoons olive oil

FOR EACH PORTION

1 ripe peach or nectarine

balsamic vinegar

1 heaping tablespoon plain yogurt

1 tablespoon whole almonds

Preheat the oven to 350°F. Line a 6-cup loaf pan with a scrunched sheet of wet parchment paper. Make a cup of Earl Grey tea with 6 tablespoons of boiling water, removing the teabag after 3 minutes. In a food processor, blitz the dried banana, pitted dates, pecans, flours, baking powder, and a pinch of sea salt until finely chopped. Add the peeled bananas, eggs, syrup, oil, and Earl Grey tea, and blitz again until combined.

Tip the mixture into your prepared pan, give it a light tap to flatten the top, pull the paper up at the sides so it's nice and even, then bake for 50 to 55 minutes, or until nicely golden and an inserted skewer comes out clean. Gently lift the bread out of the pan and transfer to a wire rack to cool.

To serve, I like to toast two slices of banana bread per portion, then serve with a halved and pitted peach or nectarine that's been grilled on a hot grill pan to bring out all that wonderful natural sweetness, then tossed in a drizzle of balsamic vinegar (you could even add a drizzle of manuka honey too). Add a dollop of yogurt, a sprinkling of crushed, toasted almonds, and tuck on in. A scattering of fresh baby mint leaves would also be delicious. Store any extra portions in an airtight container, where it will keep for 2 to 3 days.

> If you can't find whole-grain self-rising flour, you can add 2 teaspoons of baking powder per 1 cup of regular whole-wheat flour and sift well—in which case, don't add the additional baking powder listed in the ingredients.

CALORIES	FAT	SAT FAT	PROTEIN	CARBS	SUGAR	FIBER	1 HOUR 10 MINUTES
389kcal	19.6g	2.8g	9.8g	44.6g	25.6g	4.7g	

LUNCH

Lunch is a really important meal for me, especially when I'm at work. Essentially it's our opportunity to keep our energy levels up, keeping us focused and helping us get the most out of the rest of the day. You'll find a wide range of tasty meals in this chapter: all of them are straightforward and quick to rustle up, and some can be made ahead, boxed up, and taken to work to be enjoyed at your leisure. All the recipes have a nice mix of the food groups and are less than 600 calories per portion—the dinner recipes are the same, meaning you can mix things up between the chapters, if you feel like widening your repertoire.

TASTY FISH TACOS
GAME-CHANGING KIWI, LIME & CHILE SALSA

— Just one haddock fillet provides us with a source of seven different essential vitamins and minerals, plus this colorful dish gives us three of our 5-a-day —

SERVES 2

¾ cup all-purpose whole-grain flour

2 ripe kiwifruit

4 scallions

1 fresh jalapeño or green chile

1 bunch of fresh cilantro (1 oz)

2 limes

Tabasco chipotle sauce

¼ of a small red cabbage (5 oz)

1 tablespoon red wine vinegar

½ an orange

1 red or yellow pepper

2 x 4-oz fillets of firm white fish, such as haddock, skin on, scaled, and pin-boned

olive oil

2 tablespoons plain yogurt

In a bowl, mix the flour and a pinch of sea salt with ¼ cup of water to form a dough. Knead for a couple of minutes, then put aside. Peel the kiwifruit, cut in half, and put into a large, dry non-stick frying pan on a medium heat with the green halves of the scallions and the seeded chile. Lightly scald it all, turning every now and again, then place in a blender with half the cilantro, the juice of 1 lime, and a few shakes of chipotle Tabasco. Blitz until smooth, then taste and season to perfection. Very finely slice the red cabbage, ideally on a mandolin (use the guard!), scrunch with the remaining cilantro leaves and the vinegar and orange juice, then season to perfection.

To make your tacos, divide the dough into four balls and roll out each one thinly. Cook each through in a non-stick pan for just 1 minute on each side until soft, turning when you see bubbles. Cover with a kitchen towel to keep warm.

Slice up the whites of the scallions. Seed the pepper and cut into ½-inch dice. Slice the fish into ¾-inch strips, then toss with the scallions, pepper, and 1 tablespoon of oil. Return the pan you used for your tacos to a high heat and cook the fish mixture for around 4 minutes, or until the fish is cooked through and lightly golden. Divide the yogurt, fish, and veg between your warm tacos. Serve with the dressed red cabbage, that killer salsa, and lime wedges for squeezing over, then devour!

CALORIES	FAT	SAT FAT	PROTEIN	CARBS	SUGAR	FIBER	35 MINUTES
418kcal	10.6g	1.8g	35.2g	48.3g	16.8g	8.4g	

ASIAN CRISPY BEEF
BROWN RICE NOODLES & LOADSA SALAD

— Beef is packed with zinc, which we need in order to make DNA and to metabolize
key vitamins and minerals, enabling us to utilize the best of what we eat —

SERVES 2

1 tablespoon unsalted peanuts

2 cloves of garlic

2-inch piece of fresh gingerroot

sesame oil

2 star anise

7 oz lean ground beef

1 teaspoon liquid honey

1 teaspoon fish sauce

1 teaspoon reduced-sodium
soy sauce

2 limes

5 oz brown rice noodles

2 scallions

1 fresh red chile

7 oz fresh mixed salad veg,
such as bibb lettuce, carrots,
radishes, cress, spinach

4 sprigs of fresh cilantro

Lightly toast the peanuts in a dry frying pan, then crush in a pestle and mortar and put aside. Peel and finely chop the garlic and ginger. Put 1 tablespoon of sesame oil and the star anise into the frying pan on a medium-high heat. Add the ground beef, breaking it apart with a wooden spoon, followed by half the garlic and ginger, and the honey. Stir-fry for 5 minutes to crisp up and get golden brown. Meanwhile, crush the remaining garlic and ginger into a paste in the pestle and mortar, then muddle in the fish and soy sauces and lime juice to make a dressing. Cook the noodles according to the package instructions. Trim the scallions, then finely slice with the chile (seed if you like). Prep the salad veg, breaking the lettuce leaves apart and matchsticking or finely slicing any crunchy veg so it's all a pleasure to eat.

Load up your plates with that lovely salad veg, then drain and add the noodles. Spoon over the dressing, sprinkle over the crispy beef, chile, scallions, and crushed peanuts, pick over the cilantro leaves, and tuck in.

CALORIES	FAT	SAT FAT	PROTEIN	CARBS	SUGAR	FIBER	25 MINUTES
440kcal	20.3g	6g	27.5g	37.8g	10.7g	2.8g	

HAPPINESS PASTA
SWEET TOMATO, EGGPLANT & RICOTTA

— As well as being very low in saturated fat compared to most other cheeses, ricotta is also —
high in calcium, a nutrient vital in keeping our teeth and bones nice and strong

SERVES 4

2 eggplants

1–2 fresh red chiles

⅓ cup pine nuts

2 cloves of garlic

1 bunch of fresh basil (1 oz)

olive oil

2 x 14-oz cans of plum tomatoes

10 oz dried whole-wheat fusilli

7 oz ricotta cheese

⅓ oz Parmesan cheese

Sit a double-layer bamboo steamer over a large pan of boiling salted water. Halve the eggplants lengthwise and add to the baskets skin-side up with the whole chiles. Cover and steam for 25 minutes, or until soft and tender, then remove. Transfer the chiles to a small bowl and cover with plastic wrap.

Lightly toast the pine nuts in a large casserole pan on a medium heat, then lightly crush in a pestle and mortar. Peel and finely slice the garlic and finely chop the basil stalks, then add to the pan with 1 tablespoon of oil and return to the heat to cook until golden. Tip the tomatoes into the pan through your hands, crushing and scrunching them up as you go. Fill each can with water, swirl it around, and add to the pan with a good pinch of sea salt and black pepper. Bring to a boil, then simmer gently for 30 minutes, or until reduced by half, roughly chopping and adding the eggplants for the last 10 minutes.

Meanwhile, cook the pasta in the pan of boiling salted water according to the package instructions, then drain, reserving a cupful of cooking water. Peel and seed the chiles, then finely chop and stir into the sauce. Tear in most of the basil leaves and season to perfection. Toss the pasta and ricotta through the sauce, loosening with a little reserved water if needed. Serve with the pine nuts and remaining basil leaves scattered over, with a grating of Parmesan.

CALORIES	FAT	SAT FAT	PROTEIN	CARBS	SUGAR	FIBER	1 HOUR
472kcal	18.9g	5.3g	20.5g	60.2g	12g	10g	

ORANGE GARDEN SALAD
BRESAOLA & GIANT RYE CRISPBREADS

— Hunt down these giant rye crispbreads, they're fantastic—plus, rye is a great source of —
zinc, which is good for cognitive function and helps keep our nails and skin healthy

SERVES 2

1 orange

extra virgin olive oil

red wine vinegar

½ a red onion

1 handful of enoki or chestnut
    mushrooms

½ a bunch of fresh Italian
    parsley (½ oz)

1 red endive

2 large handfuls of mixed
    watercress and arugula

1 giant rye crispbread

¾ oz Parmesan cheese

6 thin slices of bresaola

Top and tail the orange, then, standing it on its flat bottom, trim off the peel. Segment the orange into a bowl, squeezing the juice from the center over the top. Add a pinch of sea salt and black pepper and 1 tablespoon each of oil and vinegar. Peel and very finely slice the red onion, ideally on a mandolin (use the guard!), pick apart or slice the mushrooms, pick and finely chop the parsley leaves, then add it all to the bowl and mix together well.

Finely slice the stalk end of the endive, going about halfway up, then pull apart the more delicate whole leaves and place gently on top of the salad with the watercress and arugula, tossing together only moments before serving.

Using your giant crispbread as a plate (you can use smaller ones and just divide the topping between them, if that's what you've got), arrange the salad on top, then use a vegetable peeler to shave over the Parmesan. Arrange the bresaola over the top in waves, then serve. Simple, vibrant, easy, and delicious.

CALORIES	FAT	SAT FAT	PROTEIN	CARBS	SUGAR	FIBER	
329kcal	10.7g	3.2g	15.8g	45.9g	13g	3.6g	15 MINUTES

HEALTHY CHICKEN CAESAR
AWESOME SHREDDED SALAD & CROUTONS

Finely sliced cauliflower isn't just delicious—when it's eaten raw we get twice as much vitamin B6 and three times as much potassium, keeping our nervous systems healthy

SERVES 2

1 lemon

½ oz Parmesan cheese

2 anchovy fillets in oil

4 heaping tablespoons plain
  yogurt

½ teaspoon English mustard

1 teaspoon Worcestershire sauce

white wine vinegar

extra virgin olive oil

1 small red onion

½ a small cauliflower (10 oz)

1 romaine lettuce

olive oil

1 sprig of fresh rosemary

2 x 4-oz boneless, skinless
  chicken breasts

1 thick slice of whole-grain bread

Finely grate the lemon zest and Parmesan into a large bowl. Slice and add the anchovies, along with the yogurt, mustard, and Worcestershire sauce. Squeeze in half the lemon juice, add 1 tablespoon of vinegar and 2 tablespoons of extra virgin olive oil, and mix to make your dressing.

Now you're going to turn regular salad into a thing of beauty by either taking your time with good knife skills or, ideally, investing in a mandolin for ease, elegance, and accuracy (use the guard!). Start by peeling and very finely slicing the red onion, then stir it through the dressing. Pull off and discard any tatty outer leaves from the cauliflower, then very finely slice it. Finely slice the lettuce by hand and pile both on top of the dressed onion, tossing together only moments before serving.

Put 1 teaspoon of olive oil in a frying pan on a medium heat. Pick the rosemary leaves over the chicken and lightly season it on both sides, flattening it slightly with the heel of your hand. Cook for 4 minutes on each side, or until golden and cooked through. Cube the bread and toast alongside the chicken, moving regularly until evenly golden and gnarly, removing only when super-crispy. Toss the salad together and season to perfection, slice up the chicken, and serve with a sprinkling of croutons and lemon wedges for squeezing over.

CALORIES	FAT	SAT FAT	PROTEIN	CARBS	SUGAR	FIBER	25 MINUTES
418kcal	17.5g	4.9g	43g	23.3g	12.5g	6.1g	

SPROUTING SEED SALAD
SMOKY BACON & BALSAMIC DRESSING

— Look for small sprouting seeds, which contain more health-promoting bioactive compounds —
that are reputed to help protect our cells from cancer and certain cardiovascular diseases

SERVES 2

1-2 slices of rye bread (5 oz)

1 slice of smoked bacon

olive oil

2 small cloves of garlic

1 sprig of fresh rosemary

3 tablespoons balsamic vinegar

3½ oz baby spinach

1 large or 2 small roasted peeled
  red peppers in brine

10 oz mixed sprouts, such as
  alfalfa, lentil, chickpea,
  mung bean

1 oz feta cheese

Tear the rye bread and whiz into crumbs in a food processor, then toast in a large non-stick dry frying pan on a medium heat until really crisp and gnarly. Once done, decant into a small dish, leaving the pan on the heat.

Finely chop the bacon and place in the pan with 1 tablespoon of oil. While it crisps up, peel and finely slice the garlic, and pick and finely chop the rosemary leaves. Toss into the pan, then, when lightly golden, remove from the heat and add the balsamic and a splash of water to make your dressing.

Pile the spinach leaves into a nice serving bowl. Finely chop the pepper, then in a separate bowl toss with all the sprouts, half the bread crumbs, and the balsamic dressing, then spoon over the spinach. Sprinkle over the remaining bread crumbs, crumble over the feta, and serve.

CALORIES	FAT	SAT FAT	PROTEIN	CARBS	SUGAR	FIBER	15 MINUTES
317kcal	8.6g	3.2g	16g	42.3g	14.2g	10.6g	

AMAZING MEXICAN TOMATO SOUP
SWEET POTATO CHIPS, FETA & TORTILLA

Sweet potato is a great non-starchy carb, so it counts towards our 5-a-day tally, plus it contains more vitamin C than regular potatoes, which our bodies need and utilize every day

SERVES 2

1 sweet potato (8 oz)

olive oil

1 teaspoon ground coriander

2 small whole-wheat tortillas

4 scallions

1 fresh red chile

½ a bunch of fresh cilantro
    (½ oz)

26½ oz ripe tomatoes

2 cloves of garlic

½ x 660g jar or 1 x 14-oz can
    of chickpeas

1 oz feta cheese

1 lime

Preheat the oven to 400°F. Wash the sweet potato, trim a ½-inch slice off the side to give you a flat edge to rest it on, then carefully cut it all lengthwise into ½-inch slices, and again into ½-inch chips. Toss with 1 teaspoon of oil and the ground coriander, then season lightly with sea salt and black pepper. Roast for 30 to 35 minutes, or until tender and caramelized at the edges. Place the tortillas in the oven for the last 5 minutes to crisp up.

Meanwhile, trim the scallions and finely slice with the chile (seed if you like) and the cilantro stalks. Remove the cores from the tomatoes and cut them into quarters. Put half the whites of the scallions, half the chile, and the cilantro leaves aside on a small plate, then place the rest in a large casserole pan on a medium-high heat with 2 teaspoons of oil. Crush in the garlic, fry for 2 minutes, then add the tomatoes. Tip in the chickpeas and their juice, top up with 2½ cups of boiling water, and put the lid on. Simmer for 20 minutes, then season to perfection. Mash up the tomatoes, then keep warm over the lowest heat until the sweet potato chips are done.

To serve, smash the crispy tortillas into the soup, add the sweet potato chips and half the cilantro leaves, and gently mix together—the tortillas will suck up the lovely juices, giving that perfectly soggy texture. Season to perfection, then coarsely grate over the feta, sprinkle with the reserved scallions and chile and the rest of the cilantro leaves, and serve with wedges of lime.

CALORIES	FAT	SAT FAT	PROTEIN	CARBS	SUGAR	FIBER	45 MINUTES
596kcal	15.6g	4.8g	24.4g	91g	23.3g	20.3g	

TOMATO & OLIVE SPAGHETTI
GARLIC BREAD & SARDINE SPRINKLES

— Protein-rich sardines are high in omega 3, and are packed with vitamins and minerals —
such as chloride, which helps us to digest our food super-efficiently

SERVES 2

4 large ripe mixed-color
    tomatoes

8 black olives (with pits)

extra virgin olive oil

½ a lemon

5 oz dried whole-wheat spaghetti

1½ oz canned sardines in oil

1 clove of garlic

dried red chili flakes

1 slice of whole-grain bread
    with seeds

¾ oz feta or ricotta cheese

2 sprigs of fresh basil

Prick the tomatoes and plunge into a pan of boiling salted water for 30 seconds, then scoop out onto a plate, saving the pan of water for your pasta. Pit the olives and tear into quarters in a large bowl, then place a sieve on top. As soon as the tomatoes are cool enough to handle, peel away and discard the skin, then cut them into quarters. Seed, placing the seedy cores in the sieve and chopping the flesh into ½-inch chunks. Push the seedy cores through the sieve so the juice dresses the olives (discard the sieve contents), then toss with the chopped tomatoes, 1 tablespoon of oil, and a squeeze of lemon juice. Taste, season to perfection, and put aside. Cook the spaghetti in the pan of boiling salted water according to the package instructions.

Pick away the spine bones from the sardines—don't worry about the smaller bones as they'll get smashed up and you won't notice them. Place in a food processor, along with the peeled garlic and a good pinch of chili flakes. Tear in the bread and blitz to fine crumbs, then tip into a dry frying pan on a medium heat. Toast the sprinkles until golden, tossing regularly.

Drain the spaghetti and toss straight into the bowl of dressing. Divide between your plates, drizzle with a little oil, and scatter over some hot sprinkles, serving the rest in a bowl on the side to add as you eat. Crumble over the feta or ricotta, pick over the basil leaves, and serve right away.

CALORIES	FAT	SAT FAT	PROTEIN	CARBS	SUGAR	FIBER	
449kcal	14.5g	3.5g	19.7g	64.3g	9g	9.6g	25 MINUTES

EASY SCANDI CRISPBREADS
PICKLED HERRINGS, RAINBOW VEG

— Protein-rich jarred herrings and fiber-packed spelt and rye flours for the Scandi crispbreads —
are all brilliant pantry staples that enable you to rustle up a quick and easy lunch

SERVES 2

1 x ¼-oz package of active dry
yeast

olive oil

1⅓ cups mixed flour (equal
parts spelt, rye, whole-grain,
bran), plus extra for dusting

1 tablespoon rolled oats

½ teaspoon fennel seeds

2 x 3-oz pickled herring fillets
(from a jar) with pickling liquor

1 small red onion

1 handful of raw crunchy veg,
such as mixed-color beets,
carrots, radishes

4 sprigs of fresh dill

2 tablespoons white wine vinegar

2 tablespoons plain yogurt

1 cup sprouting cress

cayenne pepper

Preheat the oven to 425°F. Fill a pitcher with ½ cup of tepid water, add the yeast and 1 tablespoon of oil, then mix with a fork until combined and leave for 5 minutes. Place all the flour and a good pinch of sea salt in a large mixing bowl. Make a well in the middle, pour in the yeast mixture, and mix into dough. Knead on a flour-dusted surface for a few minutes until smooth, then return to the bowl, cover, and leave for 15 minutes.

Divide the dough into two equal balls. Tear off two large squares of parchment paper and dust with flour, then roll out a dough ball between the sheets until 10 inches in diameter. Peel back the top sheet and from a height sprinkle over half the oats and fennel seeds, then replace the paper and roll again to press them in. Remove the top sheet, then transfer the dough and base paper onto a baking sheet. Repeat the process, then bake both breads for 15 minutes, or until golden at the edges and crisp, turning for the last 2 minutes.

Meanwhile, for the topping, drain 3 tablespoons of liquor from the herring jar into a large shallow platter. Peel the red onion and very finely slice with the crunchy veg, ideally on a mandolin (use the guard!). Finely chop the dill leaves, then slice the herring fillets ½ inch thick. Add all this to the platter of liquor, along with the vinegar. Gently mix together, then leave for a few minutes.

Serve the crispbreads with the pickled herring and veg (leave the salty pickling liquor behind), spooning over some yogurt and adding small pinches of cress and cayenne pepper to garnish.

CALORIES	FAT	SAT FAT	PROTEIN	CARBS	SUGAR	FIBER	35 MINUTES
595kcal	20.8g	4.4g	32.2g	75g	11.4g	19.9g	

PORTABLE JAM JAR SALADS—PART ONE

These delicious, colorful lunches will cause massive office envy. Make balanced jars by layering up carb, protein, veg, and a little dairy. Keep in the fridge and mix before serving

BOTH SERVE 1

BRITISH SALAD

Spoon **1 cup of cooked pearl barley** (⅓ cup if cooking from scratch) into the base of a 1-liter jam jar. Add **1 peeled, coarsely grated raw beet**. Grate **1 small eating apple**, mix with **2 heaping tablespoons of fat-free plain yogurt, 1 tablespoon of extra virgin olive oil,** and **1 heaping teaspoon of jarred grated horseradish,** then season to taste and spoon over the beets. Make up the rest of your jar with **1 handful each of watercress and baby spinach,** a few ripe cherry tomatoes, 3½ oz of cooked thinly sliced lean roast beef, the leaves from **2 sprigs of fresh tarragon,** and **4 smashed walnuts,** then lid on.

CALORIES	FAT	SAT FAT	PROTEIN	CARBS	SUGAR	FIBER	
539kcal	54.4g	5.1g	39.1g	40.7g	20.1g	5.4g	20 MINUTES

ITALIAN SALAD

Spoon **5 oz of cooked whole-wheat pasta** (2½ oz if cooking from scratch) into the base of a 1-liter jam jar. Halve and seed **2 large ripe tomatoes,** then whiz up in a blender with ½ **a fresh red chile,** the leaves from **1 sprig of fresh basil,** the **juice of ½ a lemon,** and **1 tablespoon of extra virgin olive oil,** season to taste, and spoon over the pasta. Make up the rest of your jar with **2 more chopped ripe tomatoes, 2 handfuls of arugula, 2½ oz of drained jarred tuna,** the leaves from **2 more sprigs of fresh basil,** and ½ **oz of shaved Parmesan cheese.** Top with **1 wedge of lemon** for squeezing over later, then lid on.

CALORIES	FAT	SAT FAT	PROTEIN	CARBS	SUGAR	FIBER	
565kcal	19.6g	4.4g	38.8g	61.7g	13.9g	10.3g	20 MINUTES

PORTABLE JAM JAR SALADS—PART TWO

Once you've got the hang of this principle, go to town mixing up your combos to embrace seasonal produce, use up any leftovers, and keep your veg drawer clean

BOTH SERVE 1

GREEK SALAD

Spoon **1 cup of cooked bulgur wheat** (⅓ cup if cooking from scratch) into the base of a 1-liter jam jar, then finely chop and sprinkle over the leaves from **2 sprigs of fresh dill**. Mix **2 heaping tablespoons of fat-free plain yogurt** and **1 tablespoon of extra virgin olive oil** together, then season to taste and spoon over the bulgur. Make up the rest of your jar with **½ a shredded little gem lettuce or heart of romaine, 4 olives** (pitted and torn into quarters), **1 sliced ripe tomato, 2 inches of sliced English cucumber, 3½ oz of shredded cooked chicken,** the roughly chopped leaves from **2 sprigs of fresh Italian parsley, ½ oz of feta cheese,** and **1 teaspoon of toasted sesame seeds.** Top with **1 wedge of lemon** for squeezing over later, then lid on.

CALORIES	FAT	SAT FAT	PROTEIN	CARBS	SUGAR	FIBER	20 MINUTES
413kcal	20.3g	4.9g	31.9g	25.9g	8.6g	4.8g	

MOROCCAN SALAD

Spoon **1 cup of cooked whole-wheat couscous** (⅓ cup if cooking from scratch) into the base of a 1-liter jam jar. Add the seeds from **½ a pomegranate.** Mix **2 heaping tablespoons of fat-free plain yogurt** with **1 tablespoon of extra virgin olive oil** and **1 teaspoon of finely chopped preserved lemon,** then season to taste and spoon over the couscous. Make up the rest of your jar with **2 inches of sliced English cucumber, ¼ of a shredded bibb lettuce, ½ a coarsely grated carrot, 1 peeled and sliced blood orange, 2 oz of drained chickpeas,** the torn leaves from **2 sprigs of fresh mint and 2 sprigs of fresh cilantro, ½ oz of feta cheese, 1 good pinch each of toasted sesame seeds, chopped pistachios, and cumin seeds,** then lid on.

CALORIES	FAT	SAT FAT	PROTEIN	CARBS	SUGAR	FIBER	20 MINUTES
598kcal	20.1g	4.6g	22g	86.3g	24.7g	14.1g	

SKINNY CARBONARA
SMOKY BACON, PEAS, ALMONDS & BASIL

Humble little peas are a source of nine different micronutrients, and are especially high
in thiamin, a B vitamin that helps our hearts to function properly

SERVES 2

7 oz freshly podded or
  frozen peas

1 tablespoon flaked almonds

1 small clove of garlic

½ a bunch of fresh basil (½ oz)

½ oz Parmesan cheese

1 lemon

5 oz whole-wheat spaghetti

1 slice of smoked bacon

olive oil

1 large egg

½ cup fat-free plain yogurt

Put a pan of boiling salted water on the heat for your pasta, dunk a sieve containing the peas into the water for just 30 seconds, then put aside, leaving the pan on the heat. Very lightly toast the almonds in a dry non-stick frying pan on a medium heat, then blitz until fine in a food processor. With the processor still running, peel and drop in the garlic, a pinch of sea salt, the basil leaves, the finely grated Parmesan, and the lemon juice. Blitz until it comes together, then pulse in the peas, to try and keep a bit of texture.

Cook the pasta in the boiling salted water according to the package instructions. Meanwhile, very finely slice the bacon and fry slowly in the frying pan with 1 teaspoon of oil on a medium-low heat until golden and crispy, then use a slotted spoon to transfer to paper towel, so the flavorsome fat stays in the pan. Scoop in three-quarters of your pea mixture to heat through.

Whisk the egg and yogurt together well. When the pasta's done, reserving a cupful of cooking water, drain the pasta and toss straight into the pea pan, mixing well, then take the pan off the heat (this is very important, otherwise the egg will scramble when you add it, and we don't want that). Pour in the egg mixture and toss until evenly coated, silky, and creamy, loosening with cooking water if needed. Taste and season to perfection, and serve topped with the remaining pea mixture and the crispy bacon. It might be skinny, but it's beautifully light and delicious. Enjoy!

CALORIES	FAT	SAT FAT	PROTEIN	CARBS	SUGAR	FIBER	20 MINUTES
493kcal	16.4g	5.2g	27g	63.6g	9.2g	11.5g	

ROASTED SWEET POTATOES
BLACK BEANS & JALAPEÑO TOMATO SALSA

Jam-packed with flavor, not only does this dish give us three of our 5-a-day, the black beans are a great source of protein, and actually contain more protein than any other beans

SERVES 2

2 x 7-oz sweet potatoes

½ cup brown rice

8 oz ripe mixed-color tomatoes

2 scallions

1 x 7-oz jar of jalapeños

½ a bunch of fresh cilantro
(½ oz)

1 red onion

olive oil

1 level teaspoon cumin seeds

1 x 14-oz can of black beans

2 heaping teaspoons cottage
cheese

Preheat the oven to 350°F. Wash the sweet potatoes, then season and roast for 1 hour, or until cooked through. After 30 minutes, cook the rice according to the package instructions, then drain. Roughly chop the tomatoes, trim and finely slice the scallions, and place both in a bowl. Tip the jalapeños and their liquor into a blender and rip in most of the cilantro, reserving a few pretty leaves. Blitz until super-smooth, then return to the jar, using 2 tablespoons' worth to dress the tomatoes and scallions (keep the rest of the dressing in the fridge for other meals).

Peel and finely chop the onion. Put a pan on a medium heat with 1 teaspoon of oil and the cumin seeds. Fry for 30 seconds, then stir in the onion and a splash of water. Cook and stir for 8 minutes, or until softened, then add the beans and all their juice. Reduce the heat and cook for a further 5 minutes until thick and oozy, stirring occasionally. Taste and season to perfection, loosening with a splash or two of boiling water before serving if needed.

Divide the beans, rice, and tomato salsa between your plates. Split open the sweet potatoes and add one to each plate. Spoon over the cottage cheese, season with black pepper, and finish with your reserved cilantro leaves.

CALORIES	FAT	SAT FAT	PROTEIN	CARBS	SUGAR	FIBER	1 HOUR
600kcal	6.8g	1.7g	23.4g	109.5g	20.8g	28.6g	

BEETS & SARDINES
HORSERADISH, YOGURT & RYE BREAD

Sardines are packed with omega-3 fatty acids, which help keep our cholesterol levels healthy and our hearts happy. They're also a great vitamin D and calcium source for healthy bones

SERVES 2

10 oz mixed-color raw
  baby beets

1 tablespoon balsamic vinegar

2 teaspoons grated horseradish
  (from a jar)

4 heaping tablespoons fat-free
  plain yogurt

8 fresh sardine fillets, skin on
  and scaled

extra virgin olive oil

1 lemon

4 sprigs of fresh dill

4 small slices of rye bread with
  seeds

Trim off and reserve any nice beet leaves, then scrub the beets clean. Cook in a pan of boiling water for around 35 minutes, or until tender, depending on their size, steaming any reserved leaves in a colander over the pan for the last couple of minutes (you could use jarred beets here instead, for convenience, in which case skip straight to the blending stage). Drain the beets, reserving a little cooking water, then put half of them (preferably purple ones) into a blender with the vinegar and horseradish. Blitz until super-smooth, loosening with a splash of cooking water if needed, then taste and season to perfection. Divide the yogurt between two plates, spread it out, and marble the blitzed beet through it—get creative!

Place a dry non-stick frying pan on a medium heat and add the sardine fillets skin-side down. Cook on the skin side only for around 4 minutes, to ensure you get mega crispy skin and soft juicy flesh—don't move them!

Meanwhile, quarter the remaining beets and toss in 1 teaspoon of oil and a squeeze of lemon juice with any steamed leaves. Divide between your plates, followed by the crispy sardines. Pick the dill leaves and sprinkle over, then serve with rye bread and a wedge of lemon on the side for squeezing over. I like it both ways, but toasted rye bread gives you an even nicer, nuttier flavor.

CALORIES	FAT	SAT FAT	PROTEIN	CARBS	SUGAR	FIBER	45 MINUTES
543kcal	21.4g	6g	51.8g	35.7g	17.8g	7.4g	

SUPER GREEN SOUP
CHICKPEAS, VEG & SMOKY CHORIZO

— When nutrient-rich kale is boiled, protective antioxidant "polyphenols" escape into the water, so using it for your soup adds extra goodness, plus we get two of our 5-a-day —

SERVES 4

1 onion

2 cloves of garlic

olive oil

1 lb potatoes

1 x 14-oz can of chickpeas

1 sprig of fresh rosemary

2 sprigs of fresh thyme

1 fresh bay leaf

4 cups really good chicken stock

5 oz kale and/or cavolo nero

3 oz quality chorizo

Peel and finely slice the onion and garlic, then put into a casserole pan on a medium heat with 1 tablespoon of oil and a splash of water. Cook for about 10 minutes, or until softened, stirring regularly.

Meanwhile, chop the potatoes into ¾-inch dice (leave the skin on for extra nutrients and fiber). Drain the chickpeas. Tie the rosemary, thyme, and bay together, then stir into the pan with the chopped potatoes and chickpeas. Cover with the stock, bring to a boil, then reduce to a simmer for 30 minutes, or until the potatoes are cooked through.

Strip the kale and/or cavolo nero off the stalks, then roughly chop. Remove the herb bunch from the pan, then add the greens and submerge for 10 minutes. Finely slice the chorizo and gently fry in a pan on a medium heat until golden, then add to the soup with any drips of spicy flavorsome fat. The kale tends to suck up a lot of the lovely stock, so top up by stirring in a good splash of boiling water just before serving, if needed.

CALORIES	FAT	SAT FAT	PROTEIN	CARBS	SUGAR	FIBER	50 MINUTES
356kcal	11.9g	3.1g	21g	42.6g	4.9g	8.3g	

HERBY PASTA SALAD
RADISHES, APPLES, FETA & BRESAOLA

The beauty of this simple dish is that all the wonderful veg gives us two of our 5-a-day, as well as a massive boost of vitamin C, providing us with more than our daily need

SERVES 4

10 oz fregola or giant
   whole-wheat couscous

1 lemon

1 orange

extra virgin olive oil

4 scallions

4 spears of asparagus

2 stalks of celery

1 zucchini

1 red pepper

1 fresh red chile

2 tablespoons sun-dried tomatoes

1 bunch of fresh mint (1 oz)

1 eating apple

1 handful of radishes

4 oz thinly sliced bresaola

1 oz feta cheese

1 pomegranate

Cook the fregola or giant couscous according to the package instructions, then drain. Squeeze all the lemon and orange juice into a large bowl and mix with 2 tablespoons of oil. Trim and finely slice the scallions and stir through the dressing. Trim the asparagus, celery, and zucchini, seed the pepper, then take pride in finely dicing it all by hand with the chile and sun-dried tomatoes (I think it's nice taking the time to do jobs like this—it improves your knife skills and is strangely satisfying).

Pick and finely chop the mint leaves, then add to the dressing with all the chopped veg and the drained fregola or giant couscous. Mix well, then taste and season to perfection. On a mandolin (use the guard!), very finely slice the apple and radishes. Plate up the herby pasta salad, arranging the slices of apple, radish, and bresaola around the plates. Crumble over the feta, then halve the pomegranate and, holding each half cut-side down in your fingers, bash the back with a spoon so that all the jewels tumble over the salad.

CALORIES	FAT	SAT FAT	PROTEIN	CARBS	SUGAR	FIBER	
474kcal	14.5g	3g	21.7g	67.3g	15.6g	5.5g	30 MINUTES

HOT-SMOKED TROUT
GREEN LENTILS, FRESH TOMATO SAUCE

— Hot-smoked trout is delicious and a great get-ahead ingredient. It's very low in saturated —
fat and is a good source of protein, helping our muscles to grow and repair

SERVES 2

2 large handfuls of mixed
  seasonal greens, such as
  chard, spinach, kale

5 oz green lentils

extra virgin olive oil

red wine vinegar

Tabasco sauce

2 x 12-oz whole hot-smoked
  trout or 7-oz skinless
  hot-smoked trout fillets (ask
  your fishmonger)

1 teaspoon grated horseradish
  (from a jar)

1 tablespoon plain yogurt

3½ oz ripe cherry tomatoes

Preheat the oven to 350°F. Tear any tough stalks off the greens. Cook the lentils according to the package instructions, steaming the greens above the pan for the last 5 minutes. Remove the greens to a board and finely chop them. Drain the lentils, toss with the chopped greens, and dress with 1 tablespoon each of oil and vinegar and a shake of Tabasco, then season to perfection. You can serve these hot or at room temperature, which is my preference. Divide between plates when you're ready to serve your fish.

Place the trout on a baking sheet and pop into the oven to warm through for 15 minutes, slightly less if using fillets. Meanwhile, stir the horseradish through the yogurt, then divide and spoon over the lentils. Put the cherry tomatoes into a blender, add a splash of vinegar, and blitz until super-smooth, then season to taste and spoon over the yogurt. Serve with the trout. Nice with some fresh whole-grain bread on the side to complete your balanced meal.

CALORIES	FAT	SAT FAT	PROTEIN	CARBS	SUGAR	FIBER	35 MINUTES
274kcal	12.1g	2.4g	27.5g	13.3g	3.9g	6.1g	

TASTY VEG OMELET
RAW TOMATO & CHILE SALSA

_ Eggs are the most brilliant source of protein—eating two gives us over a day's worth of _
vitamin B12, helping us produce red blood cells. Plus, we get three of our 5-a-day here

SERVES 2

5 oz potatoes

olive oil

1 red onion

1 red pepper

1 yellow pepper

4 large eggs

1 handful of frozen peas

2 large ripe tomatoes

½–1 fresh red chile

1 lemon

2 handfuls of arugula

½ oz Parmesan cheese

optional: Tabasco chipotle sauce

Wash the potatoes and chop into ½-inch dice, then put into a 10-inch non-stick frying pan on a medium heat with 1 tablespoon of oil and a good splash of water and toss well. Peel the onion, seed the peppers, chop both into ½-inch dice as well, then toss into the pan. Cook gently for 15 minutes on a medium-low heat, or until softened and lightly golden, adding splashes of water if needed, and tossing regularly. Meanwhile, beat the eggs with a pinch of sea salt and black pepper for 2 minutes so they're light and fluffy.

Toss the peas into the pan, then pour in the egg mixture. Use a rubber spatula to thoroughly mix it all together and begin to cook the eggs, then push it out flat, cover with a lid, and leave to cook through for 5 minutes, or until set on the top and golden on the bottom. While that cooks, halve the tomatoes and remove the cores, seed the chile, place both in a blender with half the lemon juice, and blitz until smooth, then taste and season to perfection.

Loosen around the edge of the omelet with the spatula, then place a large plate or board over the pan and in one bold, careful movement, flip it over onto the plate or board. Dress the arugula with the remaining lemon juice, pile in the center, and finely grate over the Parmesan. Serve the omelet warm with the salsa, and a shake of Tabasco chipotle sauce is nice too.

CALORIES	FAT	SAT FAT	PROTEIN	CARBS	SUGAR	FIBER	40 MINUTES
406kcal	22.3g	5.5g	22.9g	31.3g	15.7g	6.5g	

COZY SQUASH SOUP
CHICKPEA SALAD FLATBREADS

— You've gotta love butternut squash, it's such an all-rounder on the nutrition front, including — being nice and high in vitamin A, keeping our skin healthy and helping us to see properly

SERVES 6

1 large butternut squash (3 lbs)

½ a bunch of fresh thyme (½ oz)

2 heaping teaspoons harissa

olive oil

2 onions

1 fresh red chile

3 oranges

8 cups really good veg stock

1 x 19-oz can of quality chickpeas

1 large red onion

red wine vinegar

extra virgin olive oil

1 big bunch of fresh Italian parsley (2 oz)

3 tablespoons whole almonds

6 small whole-wheat flatbreads

3 oz feta cheese

Preheat the oven to 350°F. Halve the squash lengthwise, scoop out the seeds, and chop into ¾-inch chunks. Place in a large roasting pan, strip over the thyme leaves, and toss with half the harissa and 1 teaspoon of olive oil. Roast for 1 hour, or until golden and cooked through.

While the squash cooks, peel the onions and slice with the chile (seed if you like). Cook very gently in a casserole pan on the lowest heat with 1 teaspoon of olive oil and a splash of water, stirring regularly and adding more water as needed. When the squash is done, add it to the pan, finely grate in the zest of 1 orange, cover with the stock, then bring to a boil and simmer for 15 minutes. Blitz with an immersion blender until smooth, loosening with water if needed, then have a taste and season carefully to perfection.

Meanwhile, drain the chickpeas and toss with the remaining harissa in a large non-stick frying pan on a high heat. Toast until crispy and on the edge of catching, then remove. Peel and very finely slice the red onion, ideally on a mandolin (use the guard!). Place in a bowl, then top, tail, peel, and segment the oranges, adding them to the bowl and squeezing any juice from the center over the top. Add 1 tablespoon each of vinegar and extra virgin olive oil, then pick in the parsley leaves, toss together, and season to perfection.

Return the frying pan to the heat and toast the almonds, then remove and finely chop while you quickly toast the flatbreads. Fold them in half, pile in the salad and chickpeas, crumble in the feta, then roll up and squash, ready for dunking. Divide the soup between bowls and scatter over the almonds.

CALORIES	FAT	SAT FAT	PROTEIN	CARBS	SUGAR	FIBER	1 HOUR 20 MINUTES
414kcal	11g	1.5g	16.9g	63g	17g	13.2g	

SEARED TUNA
SICILIAN COUSCOUS & GREENS

— I love having fresh sustainably sourced tuna once in a while—it's easy to cook and high in selenium, which helps keep our nails and hair super-strong and healthy —

SERVES 2

4 ripe mixed-color tomatoes

1½–2 fresh red chiles

2 sprigs of fresh basil

2 lemons

½ cup whole-wheat couscous

2 cloves of garlic

1 x 8-oz piece of tuna

1 whole nutmeg, for grating

1 teaspoon dried oregano

olive oil

1 teaspoon baby capers

4 scallions

1 bunch of asparagus (10 oz)

1 large handful of Swiss chard

1 oz feta cheese

First up, a cool method to make a really flavorsome couscous—we're going to feed it with cold liquid, rather than heating it. Simply quarter the tomatoes, seed 1 chile, and place in a food processor with the basil leaves, the zest and juice from 1 lemon, a pinch of sea salt and black pepper, plus ⅔ cup of cold water. Blitz until smooth, tip the mixture into a bowl, stir in the couscous, then cover and leave aside for 1 hour to do its thing.

When the couscous has sucked up all the flavor, taste and season to perfection. Peel the garlic and finely slice with the remaining chile. Season the tuna with pepper and a few scrapings of nutmeg, then pat with the oregano and 1 teaspoon of oil. Sear in a non-stick frying pan on a high heat for 1 to 2 minutes on each side, adding the chile, garlic, and capers when you flip it, and gently jiggling it about to sear it all nicely.

Transfer the contents of the pan to a board, returning the pan to a medium heat. Trim the scallions and asparagus, then halve lengthwise, halve the chard stalks, and put it all into the hot pan with a good splash of water. Cover with a lid and steam for 4 minutes, or until just cooked through. Fluff up the couscous, crumble over the feta, pop the veg on top, slice up the tuna, and serve with lemon wedges for squeezing over.

CALORIES	FAT	SAT FAT	PROTEIN	CARBS	SUGAR	FIBER	15 MINUTES PLUS SOAKING
543kcal	13g	4.5g	45.2g	64.7g	10.4g	10.3g	

HEALTHY CHICKEN CLUB
TOMATO, LETTUCE, PEAR & TARRAGON

— Chicken is a lean protein source that's packed with B vitamins and the mineral phosphorus, which—along with calcium—makes up the matrix of our bones and teeth —

SERVES 2

1¼-inch piece of English cucumber

1 small ripe pear

2 scallions

½ a little gem lettuce or heart of romaine

2 sprigs of fresh tarragon

2 tablespoons plain yogurt

1 teaspoon English mustard

1 tablespoon cider vinegar

cayenne pepper

5 oz leftover cooked skinless chicken breast

2 super-thick slices of whole-grain bread

1 ripe beefsteak tomato

2 small handfuls of watercress

½ a lemon

Halve the cucumber and remove the watery core, then in long strokes coarsely grate the cucumber and pear on a box grater. Scrunch them in your hands to remove some of the excess juice, then place in a bowl. Trim and finely slice the scallions, shred the lettuce, pick and finely chop the tarragon (you could also use mint or basil leaves), and place it all in the bowl with the yogurt, mustard, and vinegar. Mix well, then taste and season to perfection, using a little cayenne to spice things up. Slice up the chicken.

Toast the bread in a dry frying pan until golden on both sides—placing a little weight on top will help it to color evenly and give you a great contrast between crispy outside and soft center. I like to use two super-thick slices, and once toasted, place a bread knife in between the two edges and slice the bread horizontally in half, but you could use four thinner slices if you prefer.

Finely slice the tomato and divide between two pieces of toast. Sprinkle with a little sea salt, then spoon over some dressed salad. Add the chicken and the rest of the dressed salad, toss the watercress in lemon juice and pile on top, then top with the other toasts. Skewer up some cornichons, radishes, cherry tomatoes, whatever you've got, and use them to hold the sandwiches together.

CALORIES	FAT	SAT FAT	PROTEIN	CARBS	SUGAR	FIBER	
271kcal	4.8g	1.4g	24.6g	34.2g	14.2g	6.8g	20 MINUTES

CHICKEN & GARLIC BREAD KEBABS
BLOOD ORANGE, SPINACH & FETA

Bursting with vitamin C, the blood orange's vibrant color comes from anthocyanin, an antioxidant reputed to help in the prevention of many degenerative diseases

SERVES 2

2 sprigs of fresh rosemary

2 cloves of garlic

extra virgin olive oil

1 tablespoon white wine vinegar

cayenne pepper

2 x 4-oz boneless, skinless chicken breasts

2 thick slices of whole-grain bread

8 fresh bay leaves

2 blood oranges (use regular oranges if out of season)

3½ oz baby spinach

1 lemon

1 tablespoon balsamic vinegar

¾ oz feta cheese

Pick the rosemary leaves and smash up in a pestle and mortar with a pinch of sea salt. Peel and crush in the garlic, then muddle in 1 tablespoon of oil, the vinegar, and a generous pinch of cayenne. Chop the chicken and bread into ¾-inch chunks and, in a bowl, toss and mix well with the marinade until evenly coated. Take a little care in skewering up the chicken and bread chunks, randomly interspersing them with the bay leaves on four short skewers and using hardy rosemary stalks, or wooden or metal skewers as appropriate. Of course, check that the skewers will fit inside your largest non-stick frying pan.

Place the frying pan on a medium-high heat. Lay the skewers in the pan and cook for 4 to 5 minutes on each side, or until cooked through and golden. I like to place a lid and weight on top so that the chicken makes really nice contact with the pan and gets super-crispy.

Meanwhile, top and tail the blood oranges, trim off the peel, then slice into rounds. Dress the spinach with a squeeze of lemon juice and a drizzle of oil, arrange on your plates with the blood oranges, and drizzle with the balsamic. Top with the kebabs, crumble over the feta, and serve with lemon wedges.

CALORIES	FAT	SAT FAT	PROTEIN	CARBS	SUGAR	FIBER	30 MINUTES
444kcal	12.8g	3.3g	39.2g	45g	22.3g	8.2g	

WHOLE-WHEAT SPAGHETTI
BROCCOLINI, CHILE & LEMON

Broccoli is a brilliant source of vitamin C, which we need for lots of things, one of which is keeping our immune systems in tip-top condition to help us fight illness

SERVES 2

5 oz dried whole-wheat spaghetti

2 cloves of garlic

olive oil

1 lemon

1 pinch of dried red chili flakes

4 anchovy fillets in oil

7 oz broccolini

2 heaping tablespoons
   cottage cheese

Cook the spaghetti in a pan of boiling salted water according to the package instructions. Meanwhile, peel and finely slice the garlic and put it into a large non-stick frying pan on a medium heat with 2 tablespoons of oil. Finely grate in half the lemon zest and add the chili flakes and anchovies. Fry for a couple of minutes while you trim the broccolini and split any larger stalks in half lengthwise. Add the broccolini to the frying pan with a spoonful of pasta water, then cover and leave to steam for 5 minutes, or until tender.

Use tongs to transfer the spaghetti straight from the water into the frying pan and toss together, along with the cottage cheese. Squeeze in half the lemon juice, loosen with a splash of cooking water if needed, then divide between your plates. Finish with a grating of lemon zest and a pinch of black pepper.

CALORIES	FAT	SAT FAT	PROTEIN	CARBS	SUGAR	FIBER	15 MINUTES
438kcal	17.9g	3.2g	17.9g	54.9g	5.7g	10.1g	

MEXICAN GAZPACHO
FLATBREADS & GARNISHES

— This super-refreshing dish packs in a massive four of our 5-a-day and has a very
high water content, so aids hydration, something we can all benefit from —

SERVES 2

1 large egg

1 corn on the cob

2 stalks of celery

10-oz chunk of watermelon

½ an English cucumber

7 oz ripe tomatoes

2 scallions

½ a bunch of fresh cilantro (½ oz)

½ a clove of garlic

4 oz roasted peeled red peppers
  in brine

1 tablespoon jalapeños in
  pickling liquor (from a jar)

2 limes

1 large whole-grain tortilla

1 handful of ice cubes

For your garnishes, boil the egg in a small pan of boiling salted water for
8 minutes, then drain and peel under cold water. Grill the corn on a hot grill
pan, turning regularly until nicely charred all over.

Meanwhile, trim the celery (reserving any yellow leaves) and peel the
watermelon, then roughly chop with the cucumber and tomatoes and place
in a blender. Rip in the green half of the scallions and most of the cilantro
(reserving a few leaves). Peel and add the garlic, then add the peppers and
the jalapeños with 1 tablespoon of their liquor. Finely grate in the lime zest,
squeeze in all the juice, and put aside while you finish your garnishes.

Trim and finely slice the whites of the scallions and pop on a plate with your
reserved celery and cilantro leaves. Slice the egg (preferably with an old-
school egg slicer!) and cut the kernels off the corn. Toast and tear up the
tortilla. Add it all to your garnishes plate.

Blitz the gazpacho until super-smooth, then season to absolute perfection.
Add the ice cubes and blitz again, then divide between bowls, cups, or glasses.
Serve with your plate of garnishes for dipping, dunking, and topping.

CALORIES	FAT	SAT FAT	PROTEIN	CARBS	SUGAR	FIBER	
252kcal	6.5g	1.8g	11.5g	37g	14.8g	6.8g	20 MINUTES

SUPER SUMMER SALAD
WATERMELON, RADISHES, QUINOA & FETA

— Quinoa is an awesome grain packed with many essential vitamins and minerals, as well as protein. This refreshing salad gives us four of our 5-a-day —

SERVES 4

1¼ cups regular, black, or red quinoa

4 scallions

4 oz roasted peeled red peppers in brine

1 slice of whole-grain bread

1 tablespoon Tabasco chipotle sauce

extra virgin olive oil

1 large orange

1½ oz blanched hazelnuts

1 small red onion

3½ oz radishes

1 fresh red chile

2 limes

½ a bunch of fresh mint (½ oz)

2 small red or green endive

26½-oz chunk of watermelon

3 oz feta cheese

Cook the quinoa according to the package instructions, removing from the heat 2 minutes early (this is to give you a beautiful texture when you dress it later). While it cooks, cut off the green parts of the scallions and place in a blender with the peppers, bread, chipotle Tabasco, 1 tablespoon of oil, and the orange juice. Blitz until super-smooth, then season to perfection to make a dressing. Once the quinoa is ready, drain it well, then, while still steaming hot, toss with the dressing. Toast the hazelnuts in a dry frying pan, tossing for 4 minutes, or until golden, then smash up in a pestle and mortar and, in a large serving bowl or on a big beautiful platter, fold through the quinoa.

Peel the onion, then very finely slice with the radishes and chile, ideally on a mandolin (use the guard!). Finely grate all the lime zest over the veg and squeeze over the juice, then mix together with your hands. Pick and tear over the mint leaves, reserving the pretty baby leaves for garnish.

Trim and finely slice the endive and the whites of the scallions and scatter over the quinoa. Peel and finely slice the watermelon and arrange on top of the salad. Sprinkle over the lime-dressed veg and reserved mint, then grate over the feta in long strokes. Keep it pretty or toss together before tucking in. Also nice served with a little cured meat, such as prosciutto.

CALORIES	FAT	SAT FAT	PROTEIN	CARBS	SUGAR	FIBER	45 MINUTES
474kcal	19.9g	4.6g	16.7g	61.7g	24.1g	3.4g	

ASIAN GREEN SALAD
TOFU, NOODLES & SESAME SPRINKLE

— Silken tofu is a delight to eat, a wonderful carrier of flavors, and is packed with both protein and calcium. This busload of nutritious greens contains two of our 5-a-day —

SERVES 2

1 bunch of asparagus (10 oz)

½ a head of broccoli

3½ oz sugar snap peas

7 oz silken tofu

5 oz brown rice noodles

¾-inch piece of fresh gingerroot

1 clove of garlic

2 limes

2 tablespoons reduced-sodium soy sauce

2 tablespoons sesame oil

1 tablespoon balsamic vinegar

1 sheet of nori

1 heaping tablespoon raw sesame seeds

1 teaspoon dried red chili flakes

Sit a double-layer bamboo steamer over a large pan of boiling salted water. Trim the woody ends off the asparagus, then halve the spears at an angle. Cut the broccoli into small florets, peeling and slicing the stalk. Arrange both asparagus and broccoli in the top steamer layer with the sugar snaps. Chop the tofu into bite-sized chunks and place in the bottom layer. Pop the noodles into the boiling water under the steamer. Boil and steam everything hard for 4 minutes, or until the veg are only just cooked, but still green and full of life.

Meanwhile, peel the ginger and garlic and finely grate into a bowl, adding the zest and juice of 1 lime. Mix in the soy, sesame oil, and vinegar to make a dressing. For your sprinkle, finely tear the sheet of nori into a blender, add a small pinch of sea salt and black pepper, and blitz until fine. Toast the sesame seeds and chili flakes in a dry pan until lightly golden, then tip into the blender and whiz to combine.

Reserving some cooking water, drain the noodles and toss with the veg, tofu, and dressing, loosening with a splash of reserved water if needed. Scatter over a little sesame sprinkle, keeping the rest for another day, and serve with lime wedges for squeezing over, to taste.

CALORIES	FAT	SAT FAT	PROTEIN	CARBS	SUGAR	FIBER	
459kcal	22.4g	3.9g	22.5g	41.4g	11.8g	7.7g	15 MINUTES

SEARED TURMERIC CHICKEN
HUMMUS, PEPPERS, COUSCOUS & GREENS

— Turmeric is super-high in iron—allowing our blood to transport oxygen efficiently so
we feel less tired—and contains manganese, keeping our bones strong and healthy —

SERVES 2

2 sprigs of fresh oregano

1 level teaspoon ground turmeric

olive oil

2 x 4-oz boneless, skinless
   chicken breasts

7 oz seasonal greens, such as
   baby spinach, Swiss chard

½ cup whole-wheat couscous

½ a bunch of fresh mint (½ oz)

1 lemon

1 tablespoon blanched hazelnuts

2 large or 4 small roasted peeled
   red peppers in brine

¼ x skinny hummus (see page
   230) or 2 tablespoons plain
   yogurt

optional: hot chili sauce

Pick and finely chop the oregano leaves, then place in a bowl with the turmeric, a pinch each of sea salt and black pepper, and 2 tablespoons of oil to make a marinade. Toss the chicken in the marinade and leave aside.

Blanch the greens in a large pan of boiling water until just tender enough to eat but still vibrant in color, then drain, reserving the water. In a bowl, just cover the couscous with boiling greens water, season, pop a plate on top, and leave for 10 minutes. Pick and finely chop the mint leaves and stir into the fluffy couscous with the juice of half a lemon, then season to perfection. Toast the hazelnuts in a large, dry non-stick frying pan on a medium-high heat, removing and crushing in a pestle and mortar once lightly golden. Return the frying pan to a high heat and cook the chicken for 4 minutes on each side, or until cooked through, turning halfway and adding the peppers when you flip the chicken. Reheat the greens if needed.

Meanwhile, you can either make a quick hummus (put three-quarters into the fridge for another day if making a full batch) or simply use yogurt—both options are delicious. Serve the chicken with the couscous, peppers, greens, and hummus or yogurt, scattered with the hazelnuts and with a lemon wedge on the side. Nice with a drizzle of hot chili sauce too.

CALORIES	FAT	SAT FAT	PROTEIN	CARBS	SUGAR	FIBER	30 MINUTES
579kcal	20.6g	3.2g	41.4g	58.5g	4.2g	7.6g	

SALMON CEVICHE
CHOPPED SALAD, BLACK RICE BALLS

— Salmon is a fantastic source of vitamin D, which helps keep our bones, teeth, and muscles healthy—we get it naturally from sunlight, but it's useful to top up from food too —

SERVES 2

¾ cup black rice

1 red onion

2 large lemons

1 lime

1 pomegranate

1 clove of garlic

1 fresh red chile

½ an English cucumber

½ a ripe avocado

1 handful of ripe mixed-color tomatoes

½ a bunch of fresh cilantro (½ oz)

2 x 4-oz fillets of super-fresh salmon, skin off and pin-boned (ask your fishmonger)

Cook the rice according to the package instructions, then drain and leave to cool. Meanwhile, peel and very finely slice the red onion, ideally on a mandolin (use the guard!). Place in a large bowl with 2 really good pinches of sea salt and squeeze over the lemon and lime juice (don't worry about the salt—the liquid is to cure the fish, not for drinking). Halve the pomegranate and squeeze the juice from one half through a sieve into the bowl. Hold the other half cut-side down in your fingers and bash the back of it with a spoon so that all the jewels tumble out into the liquor.

Peel the garlic, then finely slice with the chile and add to the bowl. Peel the cucumber, halve lengthwise, and use a teaspoon to remove the watery core, then slice ¾ inch thick and add to the bowl. Peel and pit the avocado and chop the same size, along with the tomatoes, then roughly chop most of the cilantro leaves and stir it all into the bowl. Chop the salmon into ½-inch x ¾-inch chunks and gently mix them into the bowl, being sure to submerge everything in the ceviche liquid. Leave for 10 minutes, to cure the salmon.

Meanwhile, use a spoon to mix and mash the rice for a couple of minutes, until it gets sticky. Wet your clean hands and roll little portions of rice into balls. Drain away most of the ceviche liquid, then sprinkle over the remaining cilantro leaves and serve right away with the rice balls.

CALORIES	FAT	SAT FAT	PROTEIN	CARBS	SUGAR	FIBER	40 MINUTES
452kcal	24.2g	4.6g	30.5g	27.1g	9.7g	7.2g	

ASIAN STIR-FRIED VEG
CRISPY SESAME NOODLE OMELET

— This is an easy, delicious, balanced way to pack in a portion of your 5-a-day. —
Eggs are our protein of choice, helping to keep us feeling full until dinnertime

SERVES 1

1½ oz brown rice noodles

2 large mixed handfuls of
   asparagus, baby corn,
   carrots, beansprouts

1¼-inch piece of fresh gingerroot

1 clove of garlic

½ a fresh red chile

sesame oil

1 teaspoon raw sesame seeds

2 large eggs

1 scallion

3 sprigs of fresh cilantro

1 lime

reduced-sodium soy sauce

Cook the noodles according to the package instructions, then drain. Trim the woody ends off the asparagus and chop up the stalks, halving the tips lengthwise to help them cook. Halve the baby corn lengthwise and match-stick the carrots. Peel and finely chop the ginger and garlic, finely slice the chile (seed if you like), and put into a ½-inch non-stick frying pan on a medium-high heat with 1 teaspoon of sesame oil. Toss for 1 minute, then add the asparagus, corn, carrots, beansprouts, and a pinch of sesame seeds. Toss and stir-fry for 5 minutes, then tip onto a plate, returning the pan to the heat.

Drizzle 1 teaspoon of sesame oil into the pan, randomly scatter in the noodles in a fairly even layer, then sprinkle over the remaining sesame seeds and leave to nicely crisp up while you beat the eggs with a splash of water. Pour the eggs over the crispy noodles, swirling them around the pan, then cover and reduce the heat to low. Leave to cook through for a couple of minutes while you trim and finely slice the scallion and pick the cilantro leaves.

Loosen the edges of the omelet with a rubber spatula and slide onto a plate. Pile the stir-fried veg in the center, then scatter over the scallion and cilantro leaves. Serve with a squeeze of lime juice and a drizzle of soy sauce.

CALORIES	FAT	SAT FAT	PROTEIN	CARBS	SUGAR	FIBER	15 MINUTES
392kcal	19.1g	4.5g	19.5g	36.6g	5g	2.5g	

SQUASH IT VEG SANDWICH
HUMMUS, AVOCADO & COTTAGE CHEESE

— This delicious hand-held veg-packed beauty gives us two of our 5-a-day, while sunflower —
seeds and cottage cheese balance the mix with some all-important protein

SERVES 2

2 whole-grain rolls with seeds

7 oz crunchy mixed seasonal
veg, such as baby carrots, raw
baby beets, cauliflower,
peppers, radishes, English
cucumber, freshly podded
peas, asparagus

1 eating apple

1 tablespoon sunflower seeds

½ a bunch of fresh dill or
mint (½ oz)

1 tablespoon balsamic vinegar

extra virgin olive oil

2 tablespoons skinny hummus
(page 230)

2 tablespoons cottage cheese

½ a ripe avocado

I like to pop the rolls into the oven and turn it on to a low temperature so they can warm through while I prep everything else.

Lay out a clean kitchen towel. Wash and trim all your veg, seeding any peppers and the apple, then pile in the middle of the kitchen towel with the sunflower seeds. Tear over the dill or mint leaves, then pull up the edges of the kitchen towel to make a bundle. Holding it firmly, bash and squash it with a rolling pin to crush up all the veg. Simply stop when you think everything is an agreeable size to eat. As crazy as it might seem, by squashing up the veg you create more surface area for the dressing to stick to, you start to break down hard vegetables, and in turn they start to release their natural juices and flavors, which makes it all taste and eat even better.

Tip the veg into a bowl and dress with the vinegar and 1 tablespoon of oil, then season to perfection. Halve your warm rolls and spread the bases with hummus and the lids with cottage cheese. Peel, pit, and finely slice the avocado and layer on top of the hummus. Pile as much of the dressed squashed veg onto the bases of the rolls as you can, pop the lids on, and squeeze together. Serve any remaining veg on the side, and get stuck in!

CALORIES	FAT	SAT FAT	PROTEIN	CARBS	SUGAR	FIBER	20 MINUTES
397kcal	17.7g	3.7g	14.1g	47.7g	15.2g	8.8g	

MY RUSSIAN SALAD
GOLDEN PAPRIKA CHICKEN

— Inspired by the popular classic and celebrating loads of veg, including two of our 5-a-day, —
I've re-worked the traditional mayo-based dressing to make it super-healthy here

SERVES 4

14 oz mixed-color raw baby
beets and small carrots

14 oz potatoes

1 bunch of asparagus (10 oz)

3½ oz freshly podded peas

2 x 6-oz boneless, skinless
chicken breasts

olive oil

smoked paprika

3 tablespoons plain yogurt

2 tablespoons cottage cheese

1 heaping teaspoon Dijon
mustard

1 tablespoon white wine vinegar

2 anchovy fillets in oil

2 cornichons

1 teaspoon baby capers

¼ of a bunch of fresh dill (¼ oz)

Cook the beets in a small pan of boiling water for around 10 minutes, or until tender. Trim the carrots, halving any larger ones lengthwise, and cut the potatoes into ¾-inch dice, then cook in a separate pan of boiling salted water for 8 minutes, or until tender. Trim the woody ends off the asparagus and slice the stalks ½ inch thick, leaving the tips whole. Add to the potato pan with the peas for 2 more minutes, then drain it all in a colander and leave to steam dry.

Rub the chicken breasts with 1 tablespoon of oil, a generous pinch of paprika, and a little seasoning, then cook for 10 minutes in a non-stick frying pan on a medium-high heat, or until golden and cooked through, turning halfway.

Meanwhile, put the yogurt, cottage cheese, mustard, vinegar, and a pinch of black pepper into a large serving bowl. Very finely chop the anchovies, cornichons, capers, and dill, add to the bowl, and mix well. Stir in the potatoes, carrots, asparagus, and peas, then taste and season to perfection. Peel and slice the beets, then fold through gently to maintain all the beautiful colors. Slice up and pile on the chicken, dust with a little extra paprika, and tuck in.

CALORIES	FAT	SAT FAT	PROTEIN	CARBS	SUGAR	FIBER	25 MINUTES
315kcal	7.9g	2g	31.3g	31.2g	11.1g	5.8g	

SESAME SEARED SALMON
TAHINI AVOCADO & SHRED SALAD

_ As well as this delicious dish giving us three of our 5-a-day, salmon is full of vitamin D, _
which our bodies need for absorbing calcium, keeping our bones and teeth healthy

SERVES 2

5 oz brown rice noodles

2 limes

2 x 3½-oz fillets of salmon,
    skin on, scaled and pin-boned
    (ask your fishmonger)

4 teaspoons raw sesame seeds

1 clove of garlic

4 teaspoons tahini

3-inch piece of English cucumber

2 small carrots

2 raw baby beets

1 cup sprouting cress

1 ripe avocado

extra virgin olive oil

½–1 fresh red chile

2 sprigs of fresh cilantro

Cook the noodles according to the package instructions, then drain and toss in a little squeeze of lime juice. Carefully slice each of the salmon fillets lengthwise into three. Scatter the sesame seeds over a board and press one side of the salmon slices into the seeds to form a crust. Place a large, dry non-stick frying pan over a medium heat, and once hot, add the salmon sesame-side down. Leave for 2 to 3 minutes, or until golden, flip over to cook for just 1 more minute, then remove from the heat.

Peel the garlic and pound into a paste with a pinch of sea salt in a pestle and mortar, then muddle in the tahini, the remaining lime juice, and a splash of water to make a wicked dressing. Use a box grater to coarsely grate the cucumber, carrots, and beets, keeping them in separate piles and dividing between two plates. Snip and divide up the cress, then divide up the noodles.

Halve, peel, and pit the avocado and add one half to each plate, then pour the dressing into the wells and add a few drips of oil. Lay the salmon alongside, then finely slice the chile and scatter over with the cilantro leaves. Toss everything together at the table and enjoy.

CALORIES	FAT	SAT FAT	PROTEIN	CARBS	SUGAR	FIBER	20 MINUTES
552kcal	33.1g	6g	28.4g	35.1g	8g	6.2g	

GRILLED CORN & QUINOA SALAD
MANGO, TOMATOES, HERBS, AVO, FETA

— Giving us two of our 5-a-day, this colorful salad also uses quinoa—it's a brilliant, —
tasty grain packed with both protein and fiber, and is also gluten-free

SERVES 4

1¼ cups regular, black, or red
  quinoa

1 small ripe mango

1 ripe avocado

10 oz ripe mixed-color tomatoes

2 limes

extra virgin olive oil

2 corn on the cob

2 cloves of garlic

4 slices of smoked bacon

1 fresh red chile

olive oil

¾ oz feta cheese

½ a bunch of fresh cilantro
  or mint (½ oz)

Cook the quinoa according to the package instructions, then drain. Peel and pit the mango and avocado, then roughly chop or slice the flesh, along with the tomatoes. In a large bowl, toss them with the lime zest and juice, 2 tablespoons of extra virgin olive oil, and a pinch of sea salt and black pepper. Leave to macerate while you grill the corn cobs on a hot grill pan until nicely charred, then carefully slice off the kernels.

Peel the garlic and finely slice with the bacon and chile (seed if you like). Put it all into a small frying pan on a medium heat with 1 teaspoon of olive oil. Stir and cook until lightly golden, tossing regularly. Tip into the bowl of macerated veg, add the quinoa and corn, and toss it all together, then taste and season to perfection. Divide between your plates, crumble over the feta, pick over the herb leaves, and serve.

CALORIES	FAT	SAT FAT	PROTEIN	CARBS	SUGAR	FIBER	25 MINUTES
438kcal	20.6g	4.4g	15.3g	51.2g	9.4g	3.3g	

DINNER

What I've set out to achieve in this chapter is the perfect balance between super-fast, get-it-out pronto recipes and medium-length recipes, for those evenings when you've got a little more time on your hands. And there's a whole host of inspiration from around the world in these dishes to really get your taste buds going. All the recipes have a nice mix of the food groups and are less than 600 calories per portion, so they can be enjoyed at lunchtime too, if that works for you. Whenever you can, take the time to sit at the table and really enjoy your meal, sharing it with loved ones if they're about.

BOMBAY CHICKEN & CAULI
PAPPADAMS, RICE & SPINACH

— Cumin and turmeric are great sources of iron, and teaming them with lemon juice like
I've done here means our bodies can absorb that all-important iron really efficiently —

SERVES 2

½ cup brown rice

½ a small cauliflower (14 oz)

½ a bunch of fresh mint (½ oz)

6 tablespoons plain yogurt

1 lemon

1 heaping teaspoon each of
   ground turmeric, medium
   curry powder

1 tablespoon balsamic vinegar

2 cloves of garlic

1¼-inch piece of fresh gingerroot

2 x 4-oz boneless, skinless
   chicken breasts

1 level teaspoon each of cumin
   seeds, black mustard seeds

4 uncooked pappadams

2 oz baby spinach

1 fresh red chile

Preheat the oven to 425°F. Cook the rice in a pan of boiling salted water according to the package instructions. Chop the cauliflower into thin wedges and place in a sieve above the rice, then cover and steam for 15 minutes. Pick the mint leaves into a blender (reserving a few baby leaves). Add 3 tablespoons of yogurt, half the lemon juice, and a splash of water to the blender, then blitz for 1 minute until super-smooth and green. Decant into a nice dish and pop into the fridge for later.

Without washing the blender, add the remaining yogurt and lemon juice, the turmeric, curry powder, and balsamic. Crush in the garlic, then peel, finely chop, and add the ginger. Blitz until super-smooth to make a marinade, then pour into a large baking dish. Lightly score the chicken breasts to increase the surface area and toss in the marinade. When the time's up on the cauliflower, tip it into the chicken dish, quickly toss together, sprinkle over the cumin and black mustard seeds, then place in the oven for 15 minutes, or until the chicken is cooked through and the cauli is gnarly.

When the rice is done, drain it, catching some of the water in the pan, then sit the sieve of rice back over the pan, cover, and place on the lowest heat to keep warm. One-by-one, puff up your dry pappadams in the microwave for around 30 seconds each. Slice and divide up the chicken, with the cauli, rice, spinach, and pappadams. Drizzle with the dressing, then finely slice and scatter over the chile. Finish with the baby mint leaves and tuck on in.

CALORIES	FAT	SAT FAT	PROTEIN	CARBS	SUGAR	FIBER	40 MINUTES
546kcal	13.1g	3.5g	48g	63.6g	13.8g	7.6g	

MEGA VEGGIE BURGERS
GARDEN SALAD & BASIL DRESSING

Tofu is a brilliant carrier of flavors, plus it's high in protein, low in saturated fat, and a great source of calcium and phosphorus, both of which make for strong and healthy bones

SERVES 4

12 oz firm silken tofu

1 large egg

½ cup whole-grain bread crumbs

2 heaping teaspoons Marmite

8 ripe tomatoes

1 tablespoon red wine vinegar

2 sprigs of fresh basil

4 soft whole-grain buns

14 oz mixed seasonal salad veg, such as English cucumber, red cabbage, apples, cress, baby spinach

½ x creamy basil dressing (see page 226)

olive oil

2 sprigs of fresh rosemary

1¾ oz Cheddar cheese

1¾ oz gherkins

Wrap the tofu in a clean kitchen towel, then squeeze and wring it out to remove the excess liquid (about 4 tablespoons should come out—it's messy, but really important to do this for great burger texture later). Place the tofu in a bowl, scraping it off the kitchen towel. Crack in the egg, then add the bread crumbs and Marmite. Mix and scrunch together really well with clean hands, then shape into 4 even-sized patties that'll fit nicely in your buns once cooked.

Roughly chop the tomatoes and put into a dry non-stick frying pan on a high heat with a pinch of black pepper, a splash of water, and the vinegar. Squash the tomatoes with a potato masher, cook for 10 to 15 minutes, or until thick and delicious, then tear in half the basil leaves and season to perfection (I sometimes add a pinch of dried red chili flakes too, for a kick). If you want to plump up your buns, pop them into a warm oven for a few minutes.

Meanwhile, finely slice or prep all the salad veg, and make the creamy basil dressing. Place 2 teaspoons of oil in a large non-stick frying pan on a medium heat. Pick the rosemary leaves into the pan in four piles, place the patties on top, and cook for 3 minutes on each side, or until golden. Slice or grate the cheese, place on the patties, reduce the heat to low, then cover and leave to melt for 3 to 4 minutes. Spread the tomato sauce onto the buns, then sandwich the cheesy burgers and sliced gherkins inside. Toss the salad with the dressing, serve alongside the burgers, and enjoy—totally awesome.

CALORIES	FAT	SAT FAT	PROTEIN	CARBS	SUGAR	FIBER	45 MINUTES
424kcal	15.7g	4.6g	24.9g	44.8g	12.1g	9.3g	

SPELT SPAGHETTI
VINE TOMATOES & BAKED RICOTTA

— Spelt spaghetti has an incredible nutty taste and is a great alternative to regular spaghetti, as it's high in wheat bran fiber, or beta-glucans, which help keep our cholesterol levels in check —

SERVES 4

olive oil

½ a bunch of fresh thyme (½ oz)

4 cloves of garlic

½–1 fresh red chile

1 lemon

1 lb ripe mixed-color cherry
   tomatoes, on the vine

8 oz best-quality ricotta cheese

11 oz dried spelt spaghetti

4 handfuls of arugula

optional: balsamic vinegar

Preheat the oven to 350°F. Pour 3 tablespoons of oil into a small bowl. Run the bunch of thyme under a hot tap for 3 seconds to reawaken it, then shake dry and strip the leaves into the oil. Peel the garlic, then finely slice it with the chile and add to the bowl. Finely grate in the lemon zest, add a pinch of sea salt and black pepper, and mix together. Lay the cherry tomatoes in a 12- x 16-inch baking dish. Rub the flavored oil all over the ricotta and place in the center of the dish, then gently rub the remaining oil over the tomatoes. Add a splash of water to the dish, place in the oven, and roast for 45 minutes, then remove. With 10 minutes to go, cook the spaghetti in a pan of boiling salted water according to the package instructions.

Lift the ricotta out of the baking dish, then shake the tomatoes off the vines, discarding the stalks. Add half a cup of pasta water to the dish and gently shake to loosen all the sticky goodness from the base. Drain the spaghetti and toss straight into the dish with a squeeze of lemon juice, season to perfection, then break that beautiful ricotta over the top. Sprinkle over the arugula, toss together well, then serve. My missus likes this with a little drizzle of balsamic too.

CALORIES	FAT	SAT FAT	PROTEIN	CARBS	SUGAR	FIBER	
492kcal	18.9g	5.8g	16.3g	61.7g	9.2g	7g	1 HOUR

SEARED GOLDEN CHICKEN
MINT SAUCE & SPRING VEG FEST

___ All the super-fresh spring veg in this dish give us two of our 5-a-day and ensure it's a really ___
nutritious meal packed with vitamin C, which our bodies need for pretty much everything!

SERVES 2

olive oil

white wine vinegar

dried red chili flakes

2 x 4-oz boneless, skinless
    chicken breasts

1 bunch of asparagus (300g)

3½ oz freshly podded or
    frozen fava beans

3½ oz freshly podded or
    frozen peas

1 bunch of fresh mint (1 oz)

¾ oz feta cheese

2 slices of whole-grain bread
    with seeds

Place 1 tablespoon each of oil and vinegar in a bowl with a pinch of chili flakes. Add the chicken breasts and massage them with all that flavor, then transfer to a medium non-stick frying pan on a medium-high heat to cook for around 8 minutes, or until golden and cooked through, turning regularly.

Meanwhile, put a large pan on a high heat and half-fill with boiling water. Trim the woody ends off the asparagus, then slice the stalks ½ inch thick, leaving the tips whole. Quickly cook in the water with the fava beans and peas for just 3 minutes. Transfer one large ladleful of veg and water to a blender, then drain the rest of the veg and divide between your serving bowls. Quickly rip the top leafy tender-stalked half of the mint into the blender, then pick in the rest of the larger leaves. Add 2 tablespoons of vinegar, a drizzle of oil, and a pinch of sea salt and blitz until super-smooth.

Place the seared golden chicken on top of the veg, spoon over the mint sauce, and crumble over the feta, then serve with a slice of bread on the side to mop up all the delicious juices. What a beautifully simple seasonal recipe.

CALORIES	FAT	SAT FAT	PROTEIN	CARBS	SUGAR	FIBER	15 MINUTES
468kcal	18g	4.2g	45.5g	32.3g	6.1g	11g	

EASY CURRIED FISH STEW
SHRIMP, WHITE FISH & SWEET TOMATOES

— Shrimp are super-high in vitamin B12, which our metabolic and nervous
systems need to function properly, plus it helps to prevent us from feeling tired —

SERVES 6

6 scallions

1 fresh red chile

2-inch piece of fresh gingerroot

olive oil

1 handful of curry leaves

1 teaspoon black mustard seeds

1 level teaspoon ground turmeric

½ teaspoon each of chili powder,
cumin seeds, fennel seeds

12 large raw shell-on jumbo
shrimp

1½ cups brown rice

8 oz ripe mixed-color cherry
tomatoes

1 x 14-oz can of light coconut
milk

6 x 3½-oz white fish fillets, such
as bream or haddock, skin on,
scaled, and pin-boned (ask your
fishmonger)

1 lemon

12 uncooked pappadams

Trim the scallions and finely slice with the chile, then peel and matchstick the ginger. Put a 10-inch shallow casserole pan on a medium heat with 1 tablespoon of oil, the scallions, chile, ginger, curry leaves, and all the spices. Stir and fry for 5 minutes, or until lightly golden.

Meanwhile, remove the shrimp heads and stir them into the pan as you go for serious added flavor, then add the rice and 5 cups of boiling water. Simmer for 10 minutes while you peel the rest of the shrimp (I leave the tails on), then use a small sharp knife to lightly score down the backs and devein them, which will mean they butterfly as they cook. Keep in the fridge until needed.

Halve and add the tomatoes to the pan, then cover with the coconut milk. Simmer for 20 minutes, then cut the fish in half across the middle and place in the pan for a further 10 minutes, or until the fish and rice are cooked through, adding the shrimp for the last 5 minutes. Pick out the shrimp heads, squeeze out all the lovely juices, then discard, and loosen the stew with a little boiling water if needed. Have a taste, and season to perfection with sea salt, black pepper, and lemon juice. One-by-one, puff up your dry pappadams in the microwave for around 30 seconds each and serve with the stew.

CALORIES	FAT	SAT FAT	PROTEIN	CARBS	SUGAR	FIBER	50 MINUTES
454kcal	15.1g	4.6g	30.9g	51.7g	4.3g	3.6g	

GOLDEN SALMON STEAKS
SWEET PEAS & SMASHED VEG

— Salmon is full of omega-3 fatty acids and is packed with vitamin D, which our bodies need in —
order to absorb and utilize calcium efficiently, keeping our bones strong and healthy

SERVES 2

14 oz mixture of carrots,
  potatoes, and rutabaga

½ a bunch of fresh chives (½ oz)

2 heaping tablespoons plain
  yogurt

olive oil

2 x 6-oz darnes of salmon, skin
  on, scaled, and bone in (ask
  your fishmonger)

1 teaspoon fennel seeds

10 oz frozen peas

1 lemon

Wash the carrots and potatoes, peel the rutabaga, then chop it all into ¾-inch chunks. Cook the rutabaga in a pan of boiling salted water for 10 minutes, then add the carrots and potatoes. Cook for another 15 minutes, or until just soft. Drain and steam dry for 1 minute, then mash. Finely chop and stir in half of the chives, along with the yogurt, and season to perfection.

Meanwhile, rub a non-stick frying pan on a medium heat with 1 teaspoon of oil, then add the salmon (you could use 2 x 4-oz fillets if you prefer). Sprinkle over the fennel seeds and cook for 6 minutes, or until golden and cooked through, turning halfway. You don't need much oil, as the natural fat in the salmon will help it crisp up, while cooking the salmon on the bone ensures it stays juicy—it's cooked when you can easily remove the bone.

Cook the peas in a small pan of boiling water, then drain and add to the salmon pan for 30 seconds, quickly shaking them around to take on some of that lovely flavor. Squeeze half the lemon juice over the salmon, and serve with the smashed veg, sprinkled with the rest of the chives, and extra wedges of lemon for squeezing over.

CALORIES	FAT	SAT FAT	PROTEIN	CARBS	SUGAR	FIBER	30 MINUTES
482kcal	21.2g	4g	42.4g	32.9g	14g	11.9g	

DELICIOUS SQUASH DAAL
SPECIAL FRIED EGGS & PAPPADAMS

Red split lentils are a brilliant source of nutrients, including iron, which we need for making blood cells to transport oxygen around the body, helping to prevent us from getting tired

SERVES 2
+ 6 LEFTOVER DAAL PORTIONS

8 cloves of garlic

2 fresh red chiles

olive oil

3 teaspoons black mustard seeds

1 heaping teaspoon cumin seeds

1 handful of curry leaves

2 onions

2-inch piece of fresh gingerroot

1 bunch of fresh cilantro
(1 oz)

½ a butternut squash (1¼ lbs)

1 lb red split lentils

3 tablespoons plain yogurt

1 lime

2 large eggs

4 uncooked pappadams

2 handfuls of baby spinach

Start by making a temper. Peel the garlic, then finely slice with the chiles, ideally ⅟₃₂ inch thick on a mandolin (use the guard!). Pour 2 tablespoons of oil into a large wide pan on a medium heat and add the mustard seeds, cumin seeds, and curry leaves for 1 minute, then the garlic and chiles. Stir so everything's flat, moving regularly until crisp and lightly golden. With a slotted spoon, remove half the temper to a plate, taking the pan off the heat.

Peel the onions and ginger and finely chop with the cilantro stalks, then chop the squash into ¾-inch cubes, leaving the skin on but discarding any seeds. Stir it all into the pan and return to a medium heat for 15 minutes to soften. Stir in the lentils, then 6 cups of boiling water. Bring to a boil, then reduce to a gentle simmer and cover for 35 minutes, stirring occasionally. Mash the squash into the daal, taste, and season to perfection. Remove 6 portions, bag them up, and, once completely cool, freeze for a rainy day when you'll be really grateful it's there, leaving the rest on a low heat to keep warm.

To serve, blitz the cilantro leaves, yogurt, a pinch of sea salt, and half the lime juice in a blender until smooth, then decant into a small bowl. Reheat the reserved temper in a non-stick frying pan on a medium-low heat with 1 teaspoon of oil, then divide into two piles and crack an egg over each. Cover and leave to slowly fry on the bottom for 2 or 3 minutes, while they coddle on top. One-by-one, puff up your dry pappadams in the microwave for around 30 seconds each. Top each portion of daal with a fried egg, and pop some spinach, dressing, pappadams, and a lime wedge on the side.

CALORIES	FAT	SAT FAT	PROTEIN	CARBS	SUGAR	FIBER	
239kcal	11.6g	2.5g	14.6g	22.3g	7.3g	3.4g	1 HOUR

ROASTED SQUASH LAKSA BAKE
CHICKEN, LEMONGRASS, PEANUTS & RICE

Squash is packed with vitamin A, which—and here's a brilliant fact—helps us see in the dark! We also use vitamin A to metabolize iron properly from the food that we eat

SERVES 2

3 sticks of lemongrass

3 cloves of garlic

4-inch piece of fresh gingerroot

2 fresh red chiles

3 scallions

1 big bunch of fresh cilantro (2 oz)

⅓ cup + 1 teaspoon coconut cream

white wine vinegar

fish sauce

1 really good chicken bouillon cube

¾ cup mixed brown and wild or brown rice

1 butternut squash (2½ lbs)

2 chicken thighs, bone in

sesame oil

1 tablespoon unsalted peanuts

1 lime

Preheat the oven to 350°F. Bash the lemongrass and remove the outer layers, peel the garlic and ginger, trim the chiles and scallions. Roughly chop it all and place in a blender. Reserving a few nice leaves for garnish, add the bunch of cilantro, along with the coconut cream and a good splash each of vinegar and fish sauce. Blitz until smooth, adding splashes of water until you have a nice spoonable consistency, to make a laksa paste.

Crumble the bouillon cube into a 12-inch shallow ovenproof casserole pan and stir in 3 cups of boiling water to dissolve it, then add the rice. Carefully slice two 1½-inch-thick rounds off the bulbous seedy end of the squash and spoon out the seeds (roast them up with a little oil and sea salt to enjoy as a snack, if you like). Remove and discard the chicken skin. On a plate, massage a third of the laksa paste (simply bag up the rest and freeze so you can enjoy big flavor—quickly—on other days) into the squash and chicken, then place them in among the rice. Drizzle with 1 teaspoon of sesame oil, then bake for 1 hour 30 minutes, until golden.

Just before serving, lightly toast the peanuts, then bash up in a pestle and mortar. Serve the laksa bake sprinkled with peanuts and the reserved cilantro leaves, with lime wedges for squeezing over. Nice with a fresh side salad.

CALORIES	FAT	SAT FAT	PROTEIN	CARBS	SUGAR	FIBER	1 HOUR 40 MINUTES
597kcal	17.9g	6g	25.8g	89.1g	16.6g	6.5g	

GOLDEN CHICKEN SKEWERS
YELLOW PEPPER SAUCE, BLACK QUINOA

___ Black quinoa contains all the goodness of regular quinoa, with the addition of vitamin E, ___
helping protect our cells from damage by stress cells known as free radicals

SERVES 2

¾ cup regular, black, or red
   quinoa

1 fresh yellow or green chile

2 yellow peppers

4 scallions

1 clove of garlic

2 tablespoons cider vinegar

olive oil

2 x 4-oz boneless, skinless
   chicken breasts

4 sprigs of fresh thyme

½ a ripe avocado

2 sprigs of fresh cilantro

optional: plain yogurt

Cook the quinoa according to the package instructions, then drain. Seed the chile and peppers, quarter the peppers, and put both into a shallow 10-inch pan on a medium heat. Trim the scallions and add the whites to the pan (reserving the green tops). Peel, slice, and add the garlic, along with the vinegar, 1 tablespoon of oil, and a good splash of water. Cover and simmer for 20 minutes, or until soft and sweet, stirring occasionally. Decant the contents of the pan into a blender, blitz until smooth, then season to perfection.

You can cook your skewers in a hot non-stick frying pan, grill pan, or even under the broiler at full whack. Slice the chicken lengthwise into ¾-inch strips, and chop the greens of the scallions into ¾-inch chunks. Checking that your skewers will fit inside your frying, broiling, or grill pan, divide up the chicken and scallions, weaving the chicken around the scallions. Strip the thyme leaves over the skewers, lightly season, drizzle with 1 teaspoon of oil, and rub all over, then cook for around 8 minutes, or until the chicken is golden, charred, and cooked through. Meanwhile, peel and slice the avocado.

Pack half the quinoa into a small oil-rubbed bowl or cup, then turn out onto a plate and repeat. Divide the yellow pepper sauce, sliced avocado, cilantro leaves, and chicken skewers between your plates, then tuck in. This is delicious with a little dollop of yogurt on the side too, if you like.

CALORIES	FAT	SAT FAT	PROTEIN	CARBS	SUGAR	FIBER	40 MINUTES
549kcal	19.8g	3.3g	42.4g	53.5g	14.6g	4.3g	

ROASTED MUSTARD MACKEREL
RAINBOW BEETS & BULGUR WHEAT

— Mackerel is a great source of omega-3 fatty acids, is super-rich in protein, and is packed with — iodine, which, through our thyroid gland, helps our metabolism to function efficiently

SERVES 2

10 oz raw mixed-color beets

¾ cup bulgur wheat

olive oil

4 x 2½-oz mackerel or trout fillets, scaled and pin-boned (ask your fishmonger)

2 teaspoons Dijon mustard

white wine vinegar

1 tablespoon rolled oats

½ a bunch of fresh thyme (½ oz)

2 large handfuls of arugula

½ a lemon

2 teaspoons grated horseradish (from a jar)

2 tablespoons plain yogurt

Preheat the oven to 400°F. Wash the beets, cook in boiling salted water for 30 minutes, or until just tender (depending on their size), then drain and leave until cool enough to handle. Meanwhile, cook the bulgur wheat according to the package instructions, and drain.

Lay a sheet of wet parchment paper in a 10- x 12-inch baking dish and rub it lightly with oil. Evenly spread the bulgur over the baking dish and place the fish fillets randomly on top. Loosen the mustard with a splash of vinegar, then brush over the skin side of the fish, and sprinkle over the oats. Remove the skin from the beets and finely slice them, ideally on a mandolin (use the guard!), then arrange them around the fish, overlapping the slices and tucking them up to and under the fillets in a nice even layer.

Mix 1 tablespoon of vinegar with 1 teaspoon of oil and a pinch of sea salt and black pepper to make a dressing. Holding the thyme like a brush, use it to dab the dressing all over the beets, then strip over the leaves. Cook at the top of the oven for 15 to 20 minutes, or until the fish is lightly golden and cooked through. Toss the arugula with a squeeze of lemon juice and sprinkle over the top. Stir the horseradish through the yogurt, season to perfection, then spoon over the fish and tuck in.

CALORIES	FAT	SAT FAT	PROTEIN	CARBS	SUGAR	FIBER	50 MINUTES
378kcal	9.4g	1g	37.4g	35.9g	13g	6.7g	

SUPER SQUASH LASAGNE
SPINACH, COTTAGE CHEESE & SEEDS

— Using whole-wheat lasagne instead of white means we get double the fiber, plus the vitamin A — we get from the squash here helps us to metabolize the iron from the spinach

SERVES 6

olive oil

1 large butternut squash (3 lbs)

1 level teaspoon ground coriander

4 cloves of garlic

1 fresh red chile

2 tablespoons balsamic vinegar

2 x 14-oz cans of plum tomatoes

7 oz baby spinach

2 oz Parmesan cheese

8 oz dried whole-wheat lasagne sheets

14 oz reduced-fat cottage cheese

6 tablespoons reduced-fat (2%) milk

1 tablespoon raw sunflower seeds

1 sprig of fresh rosemary

Preheat the oven to 350°F and rub two large roasting pans with a little oil. Carefully halve and seed the squash, leaving the skin on, then slice into ½-inch half-moon shapes. Lay in a single layer across the pans. Sprinkle over the ground coriander and a pinch of sea salt and black pepper, then roast for 50 minutes, or until soft and lightly golden.

Meanwhile, peel the garlic, seed the chile, then finely slice both and place in a large pan on a medium-high heat with 1 tablespoon of oil. Cook for 3 minutes, or until lightly golden, then add the balsamic and canned tomatoes, breaking them up as you go, and 1 can's worth of water. Simmer on a medium heat for 15 to 20 minutes, or until slightly thickened, then season to perfection.

To layer up, spread a third of the tomato sauce across the base of a 10- x 12-inch baking dish. Cover with a layer of raw spinach leaves, a layer of roasted squash, a fine grating of Parmesan, and a layer of lasagne sheets. Repeat the layers twice more, finishing with lasagne sheets. Loosen the cottage cheese with the milk, mashing the curds a little, then lightly season and spoon over the top. Finely grate over the remaining Parmesan and scatter over the sunflower seeds. Rub the rosemary sprig with oil, then strip the leaves over the top. Bake at the bottom of the oven for 45 minutes, or until golden and bubbling, then serve. Great with a lemon-dressed green salad.

CALORIES	FAT	SAT FAT	PROTEIN	CARBS	SUGAR	FIBER	1 HOUR 45 MINUTES
438kcal	13.2g	5.4g	21.2g	59g	21.6g	9.4g	

SIZZLING MOROCCAN SHRIMP
FLUFFY COUSCOUS & RAINBOW SALSA

_Adding a pop of sweetness to this dish, pomegranates are a great source of vitamin B6, keeping our nervous system healthy so our cells can send signals to each other

SERVES 2

2 sprigs of fresh rosemary

2 cloves of garlic

olive oil

1 level teaspoon smoked paprika

1 good pinch of saffron

6 large raw shell-on jumbo
   shrimp

2 oranges

½ cup whole-wheat couscous

14 oz colorful mixed seasonal
   veg, such as peas, asparagus,
   fennel, zucchini, celery,
   scallions, red or yellow peppers

1 fresh red chile

½ a bunch of fresh mint (½ oz)

1 lemon

2 tablespoons plain yogurt

1 pomegranate

Strip the rosemary leaves into a pestle and mortar, then peel and add the garlic and pound into a paste with a pinch of sea salt. Muddle in 1 tablespoon of oil, the paprika, saffron, and a swig of boiling water to make a marinade. Use little scissors to cut down the back of each shrimp shell and remove the vein. Cut 1 orange into wedges, toss with the shrimp and the marinade, and leave aside for 10 minutes.

Put the couscous into a bowl and just cover with boiling water, then pop a plate on top and leave to fluff up. Take a bit of pride in finely chopping all your colorful seasonal veg and chile, and put them into a nice serving bowl. Pick a few pretty mint leaves and put to one side, then pick and finely chop the rest and add to the bowl with the juice of the lemon and the remaining orange. Add the couscous, toss together, and season to perfection.

Put a large non-stick frying pan on a high heat. Add the shrimp, marinade, and orange wedges and cook for 4 to 5 minutes, or until the shrimp are gnarly and crisp, then arrange on top of the couscous. Dollop with yogurt, then halve the pomegranate and, holding it cut-side down in your fingers, bash the back so the sweet jewels tumble over everything. Sprinkle with the reserved mint leaves and serve.

CALORIES	FAT	SAT FAT	PROTEIN	CARBS	SUGAR	FIBER	20 MINUTES
572kcal	11.3g	2.4g	30g	91.7g	28.4g	15.9g	

ASIAN STEAMED FISH
BLACK RICE, GREENS & CHILI SAUCE

— Fresh haddock is a wonderful flaky fish that's low in both fat and saturated fat, as well as being super-high in both selenium and iodine, which help control our metabolism —

SERVES 2

¾ cup black or brown rice

1 lime

2 x 4-oz fillets of haddock or white fish, skin on, scaled, scored, and pin-boned (ask your fishmonger)

¾-inch piece of fresh gingerroot

1 clove of garlic

1 fresh red chile

2 scallions

1 tablespoon reduced-sodium soy sauce

1 tablespoon white wine vinegar

3 ripe cherry tomatoes

2 small bok choy

5 oz mixed greens, such as broccolini, asparagus, chard, kale, sugar snap peas

Cook the rice according to the package instructions, then drain. Get a pan of water on to boil that you can sit a double-layered steamer basket over later. Finely grate the lime zest over the fish fillets and place them in the base layer of the steamer, off the heat.

Squeeze the lime juice into a blender (I like to chuck the squeezed lime halves into the pan of boiling water for added steam aroma). Peel the ginger and garlic, roughly chop, and add to the blender. Seed and add the chile, trim, roughly chop, and add the scallions, along with the soy, vinegar, and tomatoes, then blitz until super-smooth. Season to perfection, then decant into a small cup or bowl and snuggle up alongside the fish.

Trim your bok choy and prep your greens, halving or quartering them lengthwise, if needed, to help them cook, and put them into the top steamer basket, above the fish and sauce. Put the lid on and carefully place the stack above the boiling water to steam for 6 minutes, or until the fish is cooked through and the greens are just done but still vibrant in color. Serve the fish, rice, and greens drizzled with your chili sauce.

CALORIES	FAT	SAT FAT	PROTEIN	CARBS	SUGAR	FIBER	40 MINUTES
416kcal	4g	0.8g	32g	66.8g	6g	4.8g	

SMOKY VEGGIE FEIJOADA
BLACK BEANS, SQUASH, PEPPERS & OKRA

Super-protein-packed black beans are a great base to this veggie version of the classic Brazilian dish, and with all the veg we get loads of fiber and four of our 5-a-day too!

SERVES 2
+ 4 LEFTOVER FEIJOADA PORTIONS

½ a butternut squash (1¼ lbs)

olive oil

1 heaping teaspoon each of ground coriander, smoked paprika

3 mixed-color peppers

2 red onions

4 cloves of garlic

4 fresh bay leaves

2 x 14-oz cans of black beans

3½ oz okra

¾ cup brown rice

2 ripe mixed-color tomatoes

½–1 fresh red chile

1 bunch of fresh cilantro (1 oz)

1 lime

2 tablespoons plain yogurt

Preheat the oven to 400°F. Halve and seed the squash, then carefully chop into 1¼-inch chunks. In a large roasting pan, toss and massage it with 1 teaspoon of oil, the ground coriander, and a pinch of sea salt and black pepper. Seed the peppers and cut into 1¼-inch chunks, then, in a separate pan, toss and massage them with 1 teaspoon of oil and the smoked paprika. Place both pans in the oven for 35 minutes, or until softened.

Meanwhile, peel and finely chop ¼ of an onion and put aside, then roughly chop the rest and place in a large casserole pan on a low heat with 1 tablespoon of oil. Crush in the garlic, add the bay leaves and a good splash of water, and cook for 20 minutes, or until soft, stirring regularly. Tip in the beans, juice and all, then half-fill each empty can with water, swirl, and pour into the pan. Simmer until the time is up on the squash and peppers, then stir both into the pan. Trim, finely slice, and add the okra, and simmer for a further 20 minutes, or until the feijoada is dark and delicious, loosening with an extra splash of water if needed. Meanwhile, cook the rice according to the package instructions, then drain.

To make a quick salsa, seed the tomatoes, then finely chop with as much chile as you like and most of the cilantro leaves. Scrape into a bowl with the reserved finely chopped onion and toss with the lime juice, then season to perfection. Remove 4 portions of feijoada, bag them up, and once completely cool, freeze for a rainy day, when you'll be really grateful it's there. Serve the remaining feijoada with the rice and salsa, a spoonful of yogurt, and a sprinkling of the remaining cilantro leaves.

CALORIES	FAT	SAT FAT	PROTEIN	CARBS	SUGAR	FIBER	
532kcal	7.9g	1.9g	19.9g	93.6g	17.6g	20.1g	1 HOUR 5 MINUTES

CRUMBED PESTO FISH
ROASTED CHERRY VINES, SPUDS & GREENS

— Juicy cherry tomatoes are high in vitamin C—protecting our cells, helping us to think properly, and really usefull here as it helps us to absorb iron from the spinach —

SERVES 2

7 oz ripe cherry tomatoes on the vine

1 slice of whole-grain bread

½ a bunch of fresh basil (½ oz)

½ a clove of garlic

1 tablespoon pine nuts

1 lemon

¾ oz Parmesan cheese

extra virgin olive oil

2 x 4-oz fillets of firm white fish, such as cod, haddock, hake, pollock, skin off, scaled, and pin-boned (ask your fishmonger)

8 oz baby white potatoes

3½ oz each of green beans, broccolini, baby spinach

1 tablespoon balsamic vinegar

Preheat the oven to 400°F. Lay the tomato vines in one side of a baking pan and pop in the oven for 10 minutes while you whiz the bread into crumbs in a food processor, then tip into a shallow bowl. Pound up the basil leaves in a pestle and mortar. Peel the garlic and add with a pinch of sea salt and the pine nuts, and keep pounding until you have a green paste. Squeeze in half the lemon juice, finely grate in the Parmesan, add 1 tablespoon of oil, and muddle together. Divide and pat the pesto all over the fish fillets, then pack on the bread crumbs. Pull the pan out of the oven and sprinkle any spare crumbs next to the tomatoes, then sit the fish on top. Halve the remaining lemon and add the wedges to the pan, then roast for 15 minutes, or until the fish is golden and cooked through.

Meanwhile, cut any larger potatoes in half, place in a large pan, just cover with boiling salted water, and cook for 15 minutes, or until tender. Place a colander above the pan, with a lid on. Trim just the stalks off the green beans, halve the broccolini spears lengthwise, and add both to the colander to steam for the last 5 minutes, adding the spinach for the final 2 minutes.

In a tray, mix the balsamic with 1 tablespoon of oil, then season to perfection. As soon as the veg are done, toss them in the tray of dressing, then drain the potatoes and add, lightly squashing and mixing them in. Serve with the fish, roasted tomatoes, and lemon wedges, with an extra drizzle of balsamic.

CALORIES	FAT	SAT FAT	PROTEIN	CARBS	SUGAR	FIBER	30 MINUTES
518kcal	23.2g	4g	37.5g	42.1g	12.5g	7.7g	

HARISSA ROASTED EGGPLANT
POMEGRANATE, PISTACHIOS, OLIVES, RICE

— With vitamin C-packed cherry tomatoes and comforting eggplant, this dish gives us two
of our 5-a-day, plus good unsaturated fat from the pistachios for happy cholesterol —

SERVES 2

1 red onion

2 cloves of garlic

olive oil

½ teaspoon cumin seeds

¾ cup brown rice

3¼ cups really good veg stock

1 large eggplant (10 oz)

2 teaspoons harissa

1 teaspoon rose water

6 olives (with pits)

7 oz ripe cherry tomatoes

1 tablespoon balsamic vinegar

2 tablespoons fat-free plain
  yogurt

½ a pomegranate

1 oz shelled unsalted pistachios

4 sprigs of fresh cilantro

Peel and finely slice the onion and garlic and place in a large shallow casserole pan on a medium-high heat with 1 tablespoon of oil, the cumin seeds, and a splash of water. Cook for 5 minutes, or until softened, stirring regularly. Stir in the rice, pour in the stock, bring to a boil, then cover and simmer for just 10 minutes. Halve the eggplant lengthwise, lightly score a criss-cross pattern into each cut side, and sprinkle with a pinch of sea salt. Loosen the harissa with the rose water then spread over each scored eggplant half and lay them on the rice, harissa-side up. Cover the pan again and simmer on a medium-low heat for 20 minutes. Preheat the oven to 350°F.

Meanwhile, pit the olives and tear into a bowl. Halve and add the cherry tomatoes, then toss both with the balsamic vinegar. When the time's up on the eggplant, remove the cover and sprinkle the dressed olives and tomatoes in and around the pan. Transfer to the oven, uncovered, for 30 minutes, or until the rice is cooked through, the liquid has evaporated, and the eggplant is beautifully gnarly and looks delicious.

To serve, spoon over the yogurt. Hold the pomegranate half cut-side down in your fingers and bash the back so the sweet jewels tumble over the top, chop and scatter over the pistachios, pick over the cilantro leaves, and enjoy.

CALORIES	FAT	SAT FAT	PROTEIN	CARBS	SUGAR	FIBER	
552kcal	21.2g	3.5g	15.6g	79.2g	16.5g	8g	1 HOUR

TASTY SAMOSAS
BEEF, ONION & SWEET POTATO

Unlike potato, sweet potato is a non-starchy carbohydrate, which means it counts towards our 5-a-day. It's also a source of other nutrients, including our forever friend vitamin C

SERVES 4

⅓ cup brown rice

olive oil

3½ oz lean ground beef

medium curry powder

1 onion

2 cloves of garlic

1 sweet potato (8 oz)

1 fresh red chile

8 sprigs of fresh cilantro

4 large sheets of phyllo pastry

optional: 1 level tablespoon
  black onion seeds

½ an English cucumber

½ a lemon

4 tablespoons plain yogurt

hot chili sauce

Cook the brown rice according to the package instructions, then drain and cool. Meanwhile, put 1 tablespoon of oil, the beef, and 1 level tablespoon of curry powder into a casserole pan on a medium heat. Stir regularly while you peel the onion, garlic, and sweet potato, then finely chop with the chile (seed if you like) and cilantro stalks. Add it all to the pan and fry for about 15 minutes, stirring often. Pour in 1½ cups of water, then simmer for 20 minutes. Crush the sweet potato with a spoon, season the mixture to perfection, and leave to cool. Stir through the rice and there's your filling.

Preheat the oven to 400°F. Normally, phyllo sheets are about 10 x 19 inches so cut each sheet in half lengthwise. Lightly brush each with a little water and evenly sprinkle over the black onion seeds (if using). Spoon an eighth of the filling at the base of each sheet. Fold and turn up the pastry to create a triangular samosa shape, using a little water to seal and stick down any overhang at the end. Place on a non-stick baking sheet and cook for 20 minutes, or until crisp and golden, turning halfway.

Scoop out and discard the watery core from the cucumber, then finely dice it and dress in the lemon juice. Serve 2 samosas per person with a spoonful of yogurt, a swirl of chili sauce, and a spoonful of refreshing cucumber. Pick over the cilantro leaves, add a pinch of curry powder, and tuck right in!

CALORIES	FAT	SAT FAT	PROTEIN	CARBS	SUGAR	FIBER	
338kcal	6.9g	1.8g	15.7g	54.7g	10g	4g	1 HOUR

VEGGIE RAMEN
WALNUT MISO, KIMCHEE & FRIED EGGS

— Wonderful walnuts are packed with vitamin E, which acts as an antioxidant and helps protect
our cells, helps us maintain healthy skin and eyes, and strengthens our immune systems —

SERVES 2

¼ of a Napa cabbage (6 oz)

1 teaspoon hot chili sauce

2 limes

¾ oz shelled walnuts

1 tablespoon white miso paste

10 oz mixed green veg, such as
    green beans, broccolini,
    snow peas

5 oz brown rice noodles

sesame oil

2 large eggs

½–1 fresh red chile

Put 4 cups of water on to boil in a large pan with a pinch of sea salt. Cut yourself a lengthwise quarter wedge of Napa cabbage. Very finely slice the top leafy half, then mix and scrunch it really well with the chili sauce and the juice from 1 lime to make a great cheat's kimchee. Cut the bottom part of the cabbage wedge in half through the stalk. Crush the walnuts in a pestle and mortar until fine, then muddle in the miso paste and put aside.

Trim just the stalks off the green beans and place the beans in the boiling water. Trim the ends off the broccolini, then add to the water with the snow peas and cabbage chunks, as well as the noodles to cook according to the package instructions. Pop the lid on until the veg are just cooked through but still vibrant in color and the noodles are tender. Meanwhile, put a non-stick frying pan on a medium heat with 1 teaspoon of sesame oil, crack in the eggs, and cover with a lid to set them on top while they fry to your liking.

Use a slotted spoon to divide the veg and noodles between your bowls. Mix the walnut miso into the greens water, bring to a boil, and spoon over the veg. Divide up the kimchee, then top with the eggs and a sprinkling of fresh chile. Serve with lime wedges for squeezing over and tuck right in.

CALORIES	FAT	SAT FAT	PROTEIN	CARBS	SUGAR	FIBER	20 MINUTES
360kcal	16.9g	3.1g	16.9g	35.7g	7.1g	5.6g	

INDIAN ROASTED CAULIFLOWER
PINEAPPLE, CHILE, CORONATION DRESSING

— Our humble but super-tasty friend cauliflower is really high in vitamin C and folic
acid, both of which aid psychological function, helping us to think properly —

SERVES 4

2 large heads of cauliflower,
 ideally mixed colors
 (2½ lbs each)

½ a medium pineapple (1¼ lbs)

olive oil

1 heaping teaspoon each of
 fennel seeds, black mustard
 seeds

1 oz sliced almonds

1 x 14-oz can of chickpeas

1 level teaspoon ground turmeric

2 level teaspoons medium
 curry powder

½ a bunch of fresh cilantro (½ oz)

1¼-inch piece of fresh gingerroot

1 lemon

2 teaspoons mango chutney

7 oz plain yogurt

1 fresh red chile

4 whole-grain chapatis

Preheat the oven to 400°F. Chop the cauliflowers into large florets, leaving any nice-looking outer leaves attached. Cook in a large pan of boiling water for 6 to 8 minutes, then drain well and tip into a large roasting pan. Peel and core the pineapple, then chop into 1¼-inch chunks and add to the pan with 1 tablespoon of oil, the fennel and mustard seeds, and a pinch of sea salt and black pepper. Toss together, then roast for 30 minutes. Turn everything over then add the almonds and drained chickpeas and cook for another 10 minutes, or until the cauli is charred and gnarly.

Meanwhile, toast the turmeric and curry powder in a dry pan on a low heat for a couple of minutes, or until smelling incredible, then put into a blender with the cilantro stalks. Peel, slice, and add the ginger, with the lemon juice, mango chutney, and half the yogurt. Blitz until super-smooth, then stir in the remaining yogurt (you can chuck it all in together, but I find that makes the dressing too thin). Season to perfection and pour over a big platter.

Pile the roasted cauliflower and pineapple mixture on top of the dressing, slice the chile and scatter over, and sprinkle with the cilantro leaves. Toss together and serve with warm chapatis for dipping and dunking.

CALORIES	FAT	SAT FAT	PROTEIN	CARBS	SUGAR	FIBER	50 MINUTES
569kcal	19.7g	5g	27.4g	71.8g	29.3g	15.2g	

ROASTED CARROT & SQUASH SALAD
MILLET, APPLE, JALAPEÑO & POMEGRANATE

Millet is super-high in a B vitamin called thiamine, which helps to keep our hearts healthy and functioning properly, plus this salad gives us three of our 5-a-day

SERVES 4

½ a butternut squash (1¼ lbs)

1 lb carrots

olive oil

1½ cups millet

1 tablespoon white wine vinegar

1 fresh jalapeño chile

1 handful of radishes

1 eating apple

1 x 12-oz jar of roasted peeled
   red peppers in brine

4 tablespoons of toasted nut mix
   (see page 228)

1 orange

2 tablespoons plain yogurt

extra virgin olive oil

½ a pomegranate

¾ oz feta cheese

Preheat the oven to 350°F. Carefully halve then slice just the bulbous seeded end of the squash ½-inch thick. Clean the carrots and cut any larger ones in half. In a baking dish toss both with 1 tablespoon of olive oil and a pinch of sea salt and black pepper. Roast for 50 minutes, or until soft and lightly golden. Meanwhile, cook the millet according to the package instructions, then drain and place in a large bowl.

Mix the vinegar and a pinch of salt in a bowl. Ideally on a mandolin (use the guard!), finely slice the chile, radishes, and apple, adding them to the bowl as you go, then toss together and pop in the fridge till needed. Drain the peppers, blitz in a blender with the nuts, orange juice, yogurt, and 1 teaspoon of extra virgin olive oil until smooth, then taste and season to perfection.

Add the roasted veg and the pepper dressing to the millet, then use your clean hands to roughly scrunch it all together until everything's vibrant and orange. Sprinkle the crunchy dressed veg on top, then, holding the pomegranate cut-side down in your fingers, bash the back of it so the seeds tumble all over the salad. Crumble over the feta and serve.

CALORIES	FAT	SAT FAT	PROTEIN	CARBS	SUGAR	FIBER	1 HOUR 10 MINUTES
517kcal	27.1g	3.9g	12.3g	56.1g	26.2g	11.1g	

CRISPY SEA BASS
PEA, MINT & ASPARAGUS MASH

— Packed with two of our 5-a-day, this super-simple supper also heroes sea bass, meaning our
meal is super-high in vitamin B12, which we need for making healthy red blood cells —

SERVES 2

10 oz potatoes

1 bunch of asparagus (10 oz)

3½ oz freshly podded peas

1 bunch of fresh mint (1 oz)

1 fresh red chile

2 handfuls of baby spinach

1½ oz strong Cheddar cheese

2 x 4-oz sea bass fillets, skin on,
scaled, scored, and pin-boned
(ask your fishmonger)

extra virgin olive oil

2 lemons

Wash the potatoes, chop into 1¼-inch chunks, and put into a medium pan of boiling salted water for 10 minutes. Meanwhile, to make the salad garnish, trim the woody ends off the asparagus. Holding the stalk ends steady, peel just 4 asparagus spears into lovely ribbons, then pop into a bowl with a small handful of the peas. Pick in just the pretty baby mint leaves, finely slice, and add the chile (seed if you like), then put aside.

Add the remaining asparagus spears and peas to the potato pan to cook for 3 minutes, then drain it all in a colander, steam dry for 1 minute, and put into a food processor. Pick in the rest of the mint leaves and add the spinach. Grate in the Cheddar, then pulse to the consistency you like (pulse because blitzing would make it gluey). Have a taste and season to perfection.

Meanwhile, sprinkle the skin of the fish with sea salt and rub all over with 1 teaspoon of oil. Place the fillets skin-side down in a cold non-stick frying pan and turn the heat to medium-high. Finely grate over the lemon zest, cover with a scrunched sheet of wet parchment paper, and cook for around 5 minutes. This is a brilliant method, giving crispy skin and flaky fish, without you having to turn it.

Divide up the mash next to the crispy sea bass, skin-side up. Toss the raw peas and asparagus ribbons with the juice from 1 lemon and 1 teaspoon of oil, then pile delicately on top. Serve with lemon wedges for squeezing over.

CALORIES	FAT	SAT FAT	PROTEIN	CARBS	SUGAR	FIBER	30 MINUTES
424kcal	13.7g	5.5g	40.6g	36.5g	5.9g	7.5g	

SPRING SQUID
PEAS, ASPARAGUS, BEANS & GREENS

— All the beautiful veg in this recipe gives us three of our 5-a-day plus over a day's worth —
of vitamin C. Broad beans are high in folic acid, which our bodies use to make protein

SERVES 2

8 oz squid tubes (ask your
fishmonger to prep them
for you)

1 onion

2 stalks of celery

olive oil

3½ oz asparagus

14 oz potatoes

1 little gem lettuce or heart of
romaine

3½ oz freshly podded or
frozen fava beans

3½ oz freshly podded or
frozen peas

2 cups really good chicken
or veg stock

1 lemon

1 fresh red or yellow chile

2 sprigs of fresh mint

extra virgin olive oil

Use a butter knife to lightly score the squid at ¼-inch intervals in a criss-cross pattern, then, with a sharp knife, slice into ¼-inch-thick strips and put aside.

Peel the onion, trim the celery, then finely chop both and put into a casserole pan on a medium heat with 1 tablespoon of olive oil and a good splash of water. Trim the woody ends off the asparagus, then slice the stalks ½-inch thick and add to the pan, reserving the tips. Peel the potatoes and cut into ½-inch dice, add to the pan, and cook it all with the lid on for around 10 minutes, or until the potatoes have softened, stirring occasionally.

Finely shred the lettuce, then stir into the pan with the fava beans, peas, and asparagus tips. Pour in the stock, then bring to a boil. Sprinkle over the squid, pop the lid on, reduce to a low heat, and simmer for 3 or 4 minutes, until the squid is brilliantly white and cooked through. Squeeze in half the lemon juice, then taste and season to perfection. Finely slice and scatter over the chile, pick and tear over the mint leaves, and finish with a few drops of extra virgin olive oil. Serve with lemon wedges for squeezing over.

CALORIES	FAT	SAT FAT	PROTEIN	CARBS	SUGAR	FIBER	
468kcal	13.1g	2.1g	34.9g	55.8g	11.2g	11.1g	35 MINUTES

CHICKEN & SQUASH CACCIATORE
MUSHROOMS, TOMATOES, OLIVES, BREAD

— This truly comforting one-pan supper contains three of our 5-a-day, and the chicken fulfills —
half of our daily vitamin B12 needs, helping us make healthy red blood cells

SERVES 4

1 onion

1 leek

4 cloves of garlic

2 slices of smoked pancetta

2 sprigs of fresh rosemary

olive oil

2 fresh bay leaves

½ a butternut squash or sweet
potatoes (1¼ lbs)

3½ oz chestnut or cremini
mushrooms

2 x 14-oz cans of plum tomatoes

1 cup Chianti or other good
red wine

4 chicken thighs, bone in

8 black olives (with pits)

7 oz whole-grain bread with seeds

Preheat the oven to 375°F. Peel the onion and cut into eighths, trim, wash, and slice the leek, peel and slice the garlic. Place a large ovenproof casserole pan on a medium heat. Finely slice the pancetta, pick and finely chop the rosemary leaves, then place both in the pan with 1 tablespoon of oil and the bay leaves. Stir regularly for 2 minutes, then add the garlic, followed by the onion and leek. Cook for 10 minutes, stirring regularly.

Meanwhile, chop the squash or sweet potato (wash first) into bite-sized chunks, leaving the skin on and discarding any squash seeds. I like to cut the stalk and face off the mushrooms because it looks nice—just add the trimmings straight to the pan, along with the whole mushrooms and chopped squash or sweet potato. Remove and discard the chicken skin and add the chicken to the pan. Pour in the wine and let it reduce slightly, then add the tomatoes and break them up with a wooden spoon. Half-fill each can with water, swirl about, pour into the pan, and mix it all together. Pit the olives, then poke them into the stew. Bring to a gentle simmer, then transfer to the oven to cook for 1 hour, or until thick, delicious, the chicken falls off the bone, and the squash or sweet potato is lovely and tender. Season to perfection, then serve with bread to mop up that tasty sauce.

CALORIES	FAT	SAT FAT	PROTEIN	CARBS	SUGAR	FIBER	1 HOUR 20 MINUTES
421kcal	12.2g	2.7g	25.2g	45.1g	17.1g	9.1g	

MOREISH FISH SOUP
MACKEREL, MUSSELS, BROTH & COUSCOUS

— Both mackerel and mussels are super-high in selenium and iodine. The latter helps —
our thyroid gland to function, in turn helping to control our metabolism

SERVES 2

2 x 4-oz mackerel fillets, skin on,
scaled, scored, and pin-boned
(ask for the head and bones too)

cayenne pepper

1 heaping teaspoon fennel seeds

1 heaping teaspoon coriander
seeds

2 cloves of garlic

1 sprig of fresh rosemary

1 lemon

2 cups really good veg stock

1 x 14-oz can of plum tomatoes

½ cup whole-wheat couscous

2 small potatoes

2 carrots

7 oz mussels, scrubbed
and debearded

½ a bunch of fresh Italian
parsley or basil (½ oz)

Put a large pan on a medium-high heat, place the mackerel head (gills removed) and bones in to brown for 5 minutes. Add a good pinch of cayenne, and the fennel and coriander seeds. Crush in the garlic, pick in the rosemary leaves, and strip in the lemon zest with a vegetable peeler. Stir and fry for 3 minutes to release all that wonderful flavor, then cover with the stock and add the canned tomatoes. Bring to a boil, then simmer for 15 minutes.

In a bowl, just cover the couscous with boiling water, pop a plate on top, and leave to fluff up. Wash the potatoes and carrots, cut into ½-inch dice, and place in a casserole pan. Sit a coarse sieve on top and pour the broth through it into the pan, using the back of a ladle to really squash and push everything through, discarding what remains. Cook the potatoes and carrots in the broth for 15 minutes, or until tender. Add 1¼ cups of boiling water and the mussels (tap any that are open and if they don't close, discard). Cover and cook for 5 minutes, or until the mussels open (throw away any that remain closed). When in season, I like to chuck a handful of freshly podded peas in too.

At the same time, place the mackerel fillets skin-side down in a dry non-stick frying pan on a medium heat with a sprinkle of cayenne. Cook for 4 minutes, or until crispy—don't move them until the time's up. Flip over for 30 seconds more, then serve on top of your couscous in large warm soup bowls. Finely chop the leafy part of the parsley or basil and stir through the soup with the lemon juice, then season to perfection and divide between your bowls.

CALORIES	FAT	SAT FAT	PROTEIN	CARBS	SUGAR	FIBER	45 MINUTES
583kcal	22.9g	4.4g	39.6g	58.3g	12.2g	8.7g	

FAGIOLI FUSILLI
SWEET LEEKS, ARTICHOKES & BAY OIL

— Protein-rich cannellini beans as well as all the micronutrient-packed tasty veggies in this comforting dish give us three of our 5-a-day, making this a great meat-free meal —

SERVES 4

2 cloves of garlic

2 carrots

2 leeks

olive oil

8 fresh bay leaves

1 x 14-oz can of cannellini beans

1 x 14-oz can of artichokes
  in water

2 cups really good veg stock

10 oz whole-wheat fusilli

¾ oz Parmesan cheese

4 sprigs of fresh Italian parsley

Peel and finely chop the garlic. Peel the carrots and chop into ¼-inch chunks, then trim, wash, and slice the leeks ¼ inch thick. Place a large casserole pan on a medium-high heat with 1 tablespoon of oil. Stir in the garlic and, a minute later, the carrot, leek, and 2 bay leaves. Add a splash of water, cover, reduce the heat, and cook for 15 minutes, or until softened, stirring occasionally.

Drain and add the beans, then drain, quarter, and add the artichokes. Pour in the stock, bring to a boil, then simmer for 15 minutes to let the flavors infuse. Meanwhile, cook the pasta in a large pan of boiling salted water according to the package instructions. Add 2 ladlefuls of the pasta cooking water to the veg pan, then drain and stir in the pasta. Season to perfection, then leave for a couple of minutes to suck up all that flavor.

Meanwhile, to make a quick bay oil, strip and tear the remaining bay leaves off their stalks into a pestle and mortar with a pinch of sea salt. Pound really well, putting some good effort in, until you have a fine green mush. Muddle in ⅔ cup of oil, then decant into a jar to keep for future use. Serve each portion of pasta with a delicate grating of Parmesan, a sprinkling of black pepper and chopped parsley leaves, and 1 teaspoon of your homemade bay oil.

CALORIES	FAT	SAT FAT	PROTEIN	CARBS	SUGAR	FIBER	40 MINUTES
496kcal	11.2g	2.4g	23.4g	74.8g	8.7g	17.8g	

SUPER-TASTY MISO BROTH
CHICKEN, MUSHROOMS & WILD RICE

Mixed wild rice is much more nutritious than regular rice and is a good source of both magnesium and phosphorus, which are good for maintaining healthy teeth and skin

SERVES 2

¾ cup mixed brown and wild or brown rice

¾ oz dried porcini mushrooms

1 red onion

sesame oil

2-inch piece of fresh gingerroot

1 heaping teaspoon white miso paste

3 cups + 3 tablespoons really good chicken stock

6 radishes

rice or white wine vinegar

1 x 7-oz boneless, skinless chicken breast

1 handful of colorful curly kale

1 sheet of nori

5 oz mixed exotic mushrooms, such as enoki, cremini, chestnut, shiitake

Cook the rice according to the package instructions. Put the porcini in a small bowl and just cover with boiling water to rehydrate them.

Meanwhile, peel the onion and cut into eighths, then place in a medium pan on a medium-high heat with 1 teaspoon of sesame oil. Cook for a few minutes, or until dark golden, stirring occasionally, while you peel and matchstick the ginger. Reduce the heat to medium-low, then add the ginger, miso paste, and stock, along with the porcini and soaking water, leaving the last gritty bit behind. Cover and simmer gently for 20 minutes. Halve the radishes, put them into a bowl, toss in a splash of vinegar and a small pinch of sea salt, and leave aside to quickly pickle.

Finely slice the chicken and tear the kale and nori into small pieces, removing any tough stalks from the kale. Break up the mushrooms, leaving the cute ones whole, and stir it all through the broth. Re-cover and cook for 4 minutes, or until the chicken is cooked through. Drain and divide the rice between your bowls, followed by the radishes. Season the broth to perfection, ladle it into the bowls, then serve.

CALORIES	FAT	SAT FAT	PROTEIN	CARBS	SUGAR	FIBER	40 MINUTES
522kcal	8.1g	1.9g	45.1g	70.4g	5.3g	5.5g	

LEMON SOLE & OLIVE SAUCE
SWEET ZUCCHINI & JERSEY ROYALS

— Zucchini and spinach contain folic acid and vitamin C, helping us to think properly, plus one lemon sole fillet gives us our daily selenium requirement for strong skin and nails —

SERVES 2

2 large mixed-color zucchini

4 cloves of garlic

extra virgin olive oil

8 oz Jersey Royal or baby white potatoes

6 black olives (with pits)

1 scallion

1 fresh red or green chile

½ a bunch of fresh mint (½ oz)

2 lemons

5 oz baby spinach

2 x 4-oz lemon sole fillets, skin off (ask your fishmonger)

Quarter the zucchini lengthwise, trim away and discard the fluffy core, then slice them at an angle around ¾ inch thick. Peel and finely slice the garlic. Put a large casserole pan on a medium heat with 1 tablespoon of oil. Add the garlic, followed a minute later by the zucchini. Stir well, then pop the lid on and cook for 15 minutes, stirring occasionally. Remove the lid, reduce the heat a little, and cook for another 5 minutes, or until sweet and delicious.

Meanwhile, halve any larger potatoes, cook in a pan of boiling salted water for 15 minutes, or until cooked through, and drain. Squash the olives and tear out the pits, trim the scallion, then finely slice both with the chile (seed if you like). Pick and finely chop the mint leaves. Toss it all in a bowl with the juice of 1 lemon and 1 tablespoon of oil to make a sauce.

Lightly squash the potatoes, then fold them into the zucchini with the spinach and lay the lemon sole fillets on top of the veg. Put the lid back on and leave to steam for 7 minutes, or until the fish is brilliantly white and cooked through—it's super-quick to cook. Plate up, spoon the olive sauce over the fish, and serve with wedges of lemon.

CALORIES	FAT	SAT FAT	PROTEIN	CARBS	SUGAR	FIBER	40 MINUTES
374kcal	16.3g	2.5g	30.2g	27.9g	7.3g	5.3g	

MIGHTY MUSHROOM CURRY
RED LENTILS, BROWN RICE & PAPPADAMS

— Mushrooms are a great source of essential B vitamins, which help our metabolisms —
function so we can utilize the energy and nutrients from the food we eat

SERVES 2

½ cup brown basmati rice

¼ cup red split lentils

1¼ cups whole milk

1 lemon

2 cloves of garlic

1¼-inch piece of fresh gingerroot

1 fresh red chile

1 tablespoon curry leaves

1 teaspoon black mustard seeds

olive oil

1 heaping teaspoon medium
  curry powder

1 onion

14 oz mixed mushrooms

8 oz ripe tomatoes

2 uncooked pappadams

Cook the rice and lentils in a pan of boiling salted water according to the package instructions (they should cook in about the same time, but there are variants, so check and adjust accordingly). Pour the whole milk (it's important that you use whole here) into a heatproof bowl with a pinch of sea salt and the lemon juice and place over the pan of rice to heat and split the milk into lumps of curds, which is pretty cool—just don't be tempted to stir it.

Peel the garlic and ginger, then finely slice with the chile and put it all into a large casserole pan on a medium heat with the curry leaves, mustard seeds, and 1 tablespoon of oil. Cook and toss for 2 minutes, until lightly golden, then stir in the curry powder. Peel and finely slice the onion and stir into the pan. Halve or quarter the mushrooms, leaving any little ones whole so you get a mix of sizes, then add to the pan with a pinch of sea salt and black pepper and a splash of water. Cook for 10 minutes, or until softened, tossing regularly. Turn up the heat and cook for 5 more minutes, or until lightly golden.

When the milk has split into curds and whey, gently pour it all in and around the mushroom pan. Slice the tomatoes and poke them into the pan, then simmer for another 5 to 10 minutes without stirring but just giving the odd shake, until the liquid has reduced down and the flavor is intense—the curds will break down slightly and become part of the sauce. One-by-one, puff up your dry pappadams in the microwave for around 30 seconds each and serve with the mushroom curry, rice, and lentils.

CALORIES	FAT	SAT FAT	PROTEIN	CARBS	SUGAR	FIBER	45 MINUTES
552kcal	18.1g	5.6g	23.1g	79.6g	18.2g	8.3g	

GREEN TEA ROASTED SALMON
GINGER RICE & SUNSHINE SALAD

_ Containing three of our 5-a-day, this recipe uses juicy mango, packed with vitamin C, _
which is important for helping to keep our immune systems in tip-top condition

SERVES 2

¾ cup brown rice

1 x 1-lb salmon tail, skin on, scaled, bone in (ask your fishmonger)

1 green teabag

sesame oil

1 clove of garlic

11 oz mixed salad veg, such as carrots, cucumber, tomato, endive

1 small ripe mango

1 lime

reduced-sodium soy sauce

1 fresh red chile

1¼-inch piece of fresh gingerroot

1 teaspoon raw sesame seeds

½ cup sprouting cress

Preheat the oven to 350°F. Cook the rice according to the package instructions, then drain. Meanwhile, score the salmon skin ½ inch deep at ¾-inch intervals and place in a snug-fitting baking dish (use one 10-oz fillet if you prefer). Season it with sea salt and black pepper and the green teabag contents, then rub all over with 1 teaspoon of sesame oil, getting it well into the cuts. Peel and finely slice the garlic, then poke a slice into each cut. Bake for 25 minutes, or until cooked through (15 minutes if using a fillet).

Prepare all your salad veg, chopping everything into bite-sized chunks or slices that will be a pleasure to eat. Slice the cheeks off the mango, then peel, slice the flesh, and put it into a nice bowl with all the veg. Really squidge and squeeze all the juice out of the mango center into a separate bowl, then squeeze in the lime juice and season to taste with soy sauce. Seed, finely chop, and add the chile to make a dressing, then toss with the veg and mango.

Peel and matchstick the ginger and put into a frying pan on a medium heat with 1 teaspoon of sesame oil and the sesame seeds. Fry for 2 minutes until starting to crisp up, tossing regularly, then stir in the rice and season to perfection. Snip the cress over the salad, and serve with the salmon and rice.

CALORIES	FAT	SAT FAT	PROTEIN	CARBS	SUGAR	FIBER	
600kcal	21.4g	3.9g	37.8g	70g	6.3g	3.9g	35 MINUTES

GRILLED STEAK & PEPPERS
HERBY JEWELED TABBOULEH RICE

— Both beef and pomegranates contain lots of B vitamins, which boost our metabolism and our nervous and immune system functions, as well as helping us feel less tired —

SERVES 2

¾ cup brown rice

½ a bunch of fresh mint (½ oz)

1 bunch of fresh Italian parsley
(1 oz)

2 scallions

1 lemon

extra virgin olive oil

½ a pomegranate

1 oz shelled unsalted pistachios

7 oz roasted peeled red peppers
in brine

1 x 7-oz filet mignon, preferably
1¼ inches thick

⅓ oz feta cheese

Cook the rice according to the package instructions, then drain and put into a bowl. Pick and finely chop the mint and parsley leaves, including any tender stalks. Trim and finely slice the scallions, then stir through the rice with the herbs, the lemon zest and juice, 1 tablespoon of oil, and a pinch of black pepper. Holding the pomegranate half cut-side down in your fingers, bash the back of it so the seeds tumble out, stir most of them through the rice, then taste and season to perfection.

Preheat a grill pan on a high heat, lightly toasting the pistachios while it heats up. Once golden, crush them in a pestle and mortar and stir most of them through the rice. Use a ball of paper towel to carefully rub the grill bars with a little oil. Drain the peppers, open them up, and grill on both sides, then remove to a plate. Rub a little oil and a pinch of sea salt and pepper into the steak, then grill for 2 to 3 minutes on each side for medium-rare, turning every minute, or until cooked to your liking. Rest the steak for a couple of minutes on top of the peppers while you pile the rice on a platter. Toss the steak and peppers in the resting juices, slice up the steak, add both to the platter, and crumble over the feta. Scatter over the rest of the pomegranate seeds and pistachios, then serve.

CALORIES	FAT	SAT FAT	PROTEIN	CARBS	SUGAR	FIBER	
597kcal	22g	5g	33.7g	69.7g	7.7g	4.1g	30 MINUTES

GINGER & CHICKEN PENICILLIN
BROWN RICE, CRUNCHY VEG & SAUCES

— Chicken is a great meat, leaner than most and high in essential B vitamins plus the mineral selenium, which among other things puts lead in your pencil, fellas—woop woop! —

SERVES 6

1 x 1.3-lbs whole chicken

4 mixed-color fresh chiles

3 x 2-inch pieces of fresh gingerroot

1 bulb of garlic

1 bunch of scallions

½ a bunch of fresh cilantro (½ oz)

1 teaspoon cider vinegar

reduced-sodium soy sauce

2 tablespoons balsamic vinegar

1 teaspoon Worcestershire sauce

hot chili sauce

2 cups brown rice

1 English cucumber

Place the chicken in your largest pot with the chiles and a good pinch of sea salt. Halve 2 pieces of ginger lengthwise. Reserving one clove, cut the garlic bulb in half across the middle. Cut the green tops off the scallions and trim the bases, putting the whites aside. Add it all to the pan along with the cilantro stalks, then top up with water to completely submerge the chicken. Bring to a boil on a high heat, then simmer for 2 hours, skimming away any fat. I sit a smaller pan lid on top of the chicken to help it stay submerged.

For the sauces, peel and finely grate the remaining ginger and the reserved garlic clove, then scrape into a bowl with any juices. Finely slice the end ¾ inch of each remaining scallion and mix into the bowl with the cider vinegar and 1 teaspoon of soy. In a separate bowl, mix 1 teaspoon of soy with the balsamic and Worcestershire sauce. Decant some chili sauce into a bowl too.

Cook the rice according to the package instructions, then drain. Meanwhile, finely slice the remaining bits of scallion lengthwise. Quarter the cucumber lengthwise and cut away the watery core, halve, then slice lengthwise again into long strips. Carefully remove the chicken from the broth and discard the skin, then slice or shred all the meat off the bone (wear gloves if you want). Divide the chicken between your warm bowls with the rice, cucumber, and scallions. Strain the broth, correct the seasoning if needed, and ladle between the bowls. Scatter over the cilantro leaves and serve with the bowls of sauces on the side. Mix everything up, then tuck in.

CALORIES	FAT	SAT FAT	PROTEIN	CARBS	SUGAR	FIBER	2 HOURS 20 MINUTES
442kcal	9.1g	2.5g	31.8g	61.6g	6.4g	2.4g	

CRAZY FISH
VEG & NOODLE STIR-FRY

— Bream is super-high in phosphorus, helping to keep the cell barriers in our bodies in tip-top condition and ensuring our cells get everything they need to function properly —

SERVES 2

sesame oil

1 heaping teaspoon Chinese
   five-spice powder

1 x 10-oz bream, scaled, gutted,
   and scored at ¾-inch intervals
   (ask your fishmonger)

5 oz brown rice noodles

2 cloves of garlic

2-inch piece of fresh gingerroot

1 fresh red chile

3½ oz broccolini

3½ oz asparagus

3½ oz baby corn

4 scallions

1 tablespoon balsamic vinegar

1 lime

reduced-sodium soy sauce

Preheat the oven to 350°F. Put a drizzle of sesame oil into an ovenproof skillet or roasting pan, then wipe it around with paper towel. Rub the Chinese five-spice and a pinch of sea salt all over the bream, inside and out, then place it in the pan—I like to sit the fish upright, as in the picture. Roast for 15 minutes, or until golden and cooked through. The fish will be juicy and flaky, while the skin crisps up and becomes a pleasure to eat.

Cook the noodles according to the package instructions, then drain. Meanwhile, peel the garlic and ginger, then slice with the chile. Trim the woody ends off the broccolini and asparagus, then roughly slice the stalks, leaving the tips whole. Halve the corn lengthwise, trim and slice the scallions.

Put a large pan or wok on a high heat. Once hot, add 1 tablespoon of sesame oil, followed by the garlic, ginger, and chile. Stir-fry for 1 minute, then add the veg for a further 2 minutes, tossing often. Toss in the drained noodles and the vinegar for another 2 minutes, allowing the noodles to just start catching. Divide between your plates, and serve with the bream, wedges of lime, and soy sauce so you can season to perfection. Have fun removing the delicious bream from the bone, and get stuck in!

CALORIES	FAT	SAT FAT	PROTEIN	CARBS	SUGAR	FIBER	
423kcal	12.3g	1.3g	35g	43g	8.6g	4.2g	25 MINUTES

PORK & APPLESAUCE
GLAZED CARROTS, BROWN RICE & GREENS

___ Pork is a great source of B vitamins and is especially high in thiamin, which we need ___
for a healthy heart. All the veg here also give us three of our 5-a-day—brilliant!

SERVES 2

2 green eating apples

½-inch piece of fresh gingerroot

¾ cup brown rice

7 oz small carrots

7 oz broccolini

7½-oz piece of lean pork fillet

1 whole nutmeg, for grating

8 leaves of fresh sage

olive oil

2 oranges

2 tablespoons plain yogurt

Quarter the apples and remove the cores, peel and finely chop the ginger, and place both in a pan with 1¼ cups of boiling water. Boil hard for 10 minutes, stirring occasionally. Tip the contents of the pan into a blender and blitz until smooth. Rinse the pan, return to the heat, and cook the rice according to the package instructions. Steam the carrots in a colander above the rice for 20 minutes with a lid on, then remove them to a plate. Add the broccolini to the colander to steam for the last 5 minutes, then put aside and drain the rice.

Meanwhile, season the pork all over with a pinch of sea salt and black pepper, finely grate over a quarter of the nutmeg, then pick over the sage leaves and really press them into both sides of the pork. Put 1 tablespoon of oil into a large frying pan on a medium heat, then add the pork and steamed carrots. Cook the pork for 4 minutes on each side (depending on its thickness—use your instincts), or until golden and cooked through.

Remove the pork to a board to rest for a few minutes. Reduce the heat to low, squeeze the orange juice over the carrots, shake the pan to coat them and pick up the sticky bits from the bottom, then leave until it becomes a natural syrupy glaze. Slice the pork and serve with the rice, broccolini, and carrots. Swirl the yogurt through half the applesauce (keep the rest for another day) and serve on the side. Drizzle with any pan and resting juices, and tuck in.

CALORIES	FAT	SAT FAT	PROTEIN	CARBS	SUGAR	FIBER	
579kcal	10.6g	3.3g	36.6g	90g	28.3g	9.2g	50 MINUTES

SNACKS & DRINKS

Snacks have that ability to totally tip our daily balance in the wrong direction, without us even realizing—it's very easy to consume a large volume of calories with little nutritional value. As delicious as some naughty treats can be, they should be enjoyed as treats, so this chapter exists to give you some alternatives that you can embrace on a regular basis. I've kept it really simple, with everything coming in at around 100 calories, so that it's super-easy to keep track of the amount you're snacking on throughout the day. Even if you can favor these choices just half the time, I'm sure you'll feel the benefits. I've also had a bit of fun celebrating humble H_2O and some tasty ways to help you enjoy it.

100-CALORIE SALAD SNACK BOWLS
PART ONE

Next time the nibbles strike, instead of hitting the cookie jar, choose one of these veg-packed salad snack bowls—the high water content of the veg will help fill you up

CREAMY BASIL DRESSING Good for 3 salad portions. Simply blitz **4 tablespoons of plain yogurt** with **1 tablespoon of white wine vinegar, 1 teaspoon of Dijon mustard**, the leaves from **4 sprigs of fresh basil, ¼ of a fresh red chile**, and a pinch of sea salt and black pepper until super-smooth.

TOASTED SEED MIX Make a batch to use here and as a snack in its own right. Simply toast a mixture of **your favorite seeds, such as sunflower, poppy, sesame, flaxseed**, in a dry pan until smelling amazing, tossing regularly. Leave them whole or lightly crush them in a pestle and mortar.

EACH SALAD SERVES 1

GEM LETTUCE, RADISH, PEA & CLEMENTINE SALAD Wedge up **1 little gem lettuce or heart of romaine** and team it with **2 quartered radishes, 1 small handful of freshly podded peas, 1 segmented clementine**, the smaller leaves from **2 sprigs of fresh basil**, and **½ tablespoon of your toasted seed mix**. Toss in **1½ tablespoons of your creamy basil dressing** just before tucking in.

BIBB LETTUCE, FENNEL, BLUEBERRY & CHILI SALAD Slice ½ a **Bibb lettuce**, pick the leafy tops off **¼ of a bulb of fennel** and finely slice it, ideally on a mandolin (use the guard!), and mix with **1 oz of blueberries, 1 pinch of dried red chili flakes**, and **½ tablespoon of your toasted seed mix**. Toss in **1½ tablespoons of your creamy basil dressing** just before tucking in.

GEM LETTUCE, CUCUMBER, APPLE & MINT SALAD Wedge up **1 little gem lettuce or heart of romaine**, slice up a **1½-inch chunk of English cucumber** and **½ a small apple**, preferably with a crinkle-cut knife, and mix with the smaller leaves from **2 sprigs of fresh mint** and **½ tablespoon of your toasted seed mix**. Toss in **1½ tablespoons of your creamy basil dressing** just before tucking in.

CALORIES	FAT	SAT FAT	PROTEIN	CARBS	SUGAR	FIBER	15 MINUTES
100kcal	4.8g	1.1g	4.8g	11.2g	9.8g	4g	

THESE VALUES ARE AN AVERAGE OF THE THREE SALAD RECIPES ABOVE

100-CALORIE SALAD SNACK BOWLS
PART TWO

These lovely nutritious little salads provide us with a good variety of essential vitamins and minerals, which the fat from the toasted nut mix helps us to absorb

CREAMY MINT DRESSING Good for 3 salad portions. Simply blitz up **4 tablespoons of plain yogurt** with **1 tablespoon of white wine vinegar, 1 teaspoon of Dijon mustard,** the leaves from **3 sprigs of fresh mint, ¼ of a fresh red chile** and a pinch of sea salt and black pepper until super-smooth.

TOASTED NUT MIX Make a batch to use here and for sprinkling on breakfasts. Simply toast a mixture of **your favorite shelled unsalted nuts, such as walnuts, pistachios, almonds, hazelnuts,** in a dry pan until smelling amazing, tossing regularly, then roughly crush in a pestle and mortar.

EACH SALAD SERVES 1

ICEBERG LETTUCE, ZUCCHINI, PEAR & DILL SALAD Slice up ¼ **of an iceberg lettuce,** peel **2 baby zucchini** into ribbons, finely slice ½ **a pear,** and mix with the leaves from **2 sprigs of fresh dill** and **1 teaspoon of your toasted nut mix.** Toss in **1½ tablespoons of your creamy mint dressing** just before tucking in.

BIBB LETTUCE, ASPARAGUS, STRAWBERRY & MINT SALAD Slice up ½ **a Bibb lettuce,** halve **5 small strawberries,** and peel **3 spears of asparagus** into ribbons, then mix with the smaller leaves from **2 sprigs of fresh mint** and **1 teaspoon of your toasted nut mix.** Toss in **1½ tablespoons of your creamy mint dressing** just before tucking in.

ICEBERG LETTUCE, BROAD BEAN, GRAPE & TARRAGON SALAD Slice up ¼ **of an iceberg lettuce** and mix with **1 small handful of freshly podded broad beans, 6 whole or halved grapes,** the leaves from **2 sprigs of fresh tarragon** and **1 teaspoon of your toasted nut mix.** Toss in **1½ tablespoons of your creamy mint dressing** just before tucking in.

CALORIES	FAT	SAT FAT	PROTEIN	CARBS	SUGAR	FIBER	15 MINUTES
100kcal	4.5g	1.1g	5.1g	10.2g	9g	3.1g	

THESE VALUES ARE AN AVERAGE OF THE THREE SALAD RECIPES ABOVE

SKINNY HOMEMADE HUMMUS

— Mighty chickpeas are high in protein, fiber, and more than ten different micronutrients,
including a hefty amount of the mineral copper, keeping our hair and skin nice and healthy —

This recipe requires you to hunt out a jar of really good-quality chickpeas—they have much better flavor, so will guarantee an amazing result. Tip **1 x 660g jar of chickpeas**, juice and all, into a blender. Add **1 teaspoon of tahini**, **2 tablespoons of plain yogurt**, **½ a peeled clove of garlic**, the **juice of ½ a lemon**, and **1 pinch of cayenne pepper**, then blitz until smooth. Taste and season to perfection, then serve with an extra sprinkling of cayenne. Pair a portion of hummus with **3 oz of raw seasonal crunchy veg crudités** for a great snack.

CALORIES	FAT	SAT FAT	PROTEIN	CARBS	SUGAR	FIBER	5 MINUTES
99kcal	2.5g	0.5g	5.9g	13.3g	0.8g	4g	

FEISTY BEET & HORSERADISH DIP

— Beautiful beets are super-high in folic acid—so they are great for any expectant ladies out
there—plus we all need folate to make protein, the building blocks of our bodies —

SERVES 4

Roughly chop **8 oz of beets** (from a jar), then put them into a blender, juice and all, with **2 heaping tablespoons of plain yogurt**, **1 pinch of sea salt and black pepper**, **1 teaspoon of red wine vinegar**, and **2 heaping teaspoons of grated horseradish** (from a jar), or, even better, a **generous grating of fresh horseradish**. Blitz until smooth, taste and correct the balance of flavors, then serve with an extra grating of fresh horseradish, if you dare! Pair a portion of this dip with **3 oz of raw seasonal crunchy veg crudités** for a super snack.

CALORIES	FAT	SAT FAT	PROTEIN	CARBS	SUGAR	FIBER	5 MINUTES
60kcal	1.1g	0.4g	1.7g	10.8g	10.1g	3.3g	

HEALTHY PAPPADAM SNACKS
FOUR TASTY TOPPING COMBOS

Gram- or chickpea-flour pappadams are gluten-free and high in protein, so when teamed
with protein-rich cottage cheese too, this snack is sure to keep hunger pangs at bay

EACH COMBO SERVES 1

CHEESE, CHILE & SEEDS

Puff up **1 dry pappadam** in the microwave for around 30 seconds. Spoon over **1 tablespoon of cottage
cheese**, ¼ of a very finely sliced fresh chile, and a little peeled **finely chopped red onion** tossed in
a squeeze of lemon juice. Scatter with **1 teaspoon of mixed poppy and sunflower seeds** and enjoy.

CHEESE, TOMATO & BASIL

Puff up **1 dry pappadam** in the microwave for around 30 seconds. Spoon over **1 tablespoon of cottage
cheese**, chop and add **1 small handful of ripe mixed-color tomatoes** and pick over **a few fresh baby
basil leaves**. Sprinkle with a pinch of sea salt, drizzle with **a little balsamic vinegar**, and enjoy.

CHEESE & MANGO CHUTNEY

Puff up **1 dry pappadam** in the microwave for around 30 seconds. Spoon over **1 tablespoon of cottage
cheese**, then loosen **2 teaspoons of mango chutney** with a splash of water and drizzle over the top.
Chop **3 sprigs of fresh cilantro**, sprinkle over with **1 pinch of sesame seeds**, and enjoy.

CHEESE & QUICK PICKLED VEG

Puff up **1 dry pappadam** in the microwave for around 30 seconds. Spoon over **1 tablespoon of cottage
cheese**. Coarsely grate ½ a small carrot and a ¾-inch piece of cucumber, scrunch with ½ a teaspoon
each of white wine vinegar and reduced-sodium soy sauce, then scatter over with **1 pinch of sesame
seeds** and enjoy.

CALORIES	FAT	SAT FAT	PROTEIN	CARBS	SUGAR	FIBER	5 MINUTES
91kcal	4.6g	1.4g	5.1g	7.9g	3.6g	1.5g	

THESE VALUES ARE AN AVERAGE OF THE FOUR RECIPES ABOVE

POPCORN FUN
LOTS OF DELICIOUS IDEAS

— Popcorn cooked this way is super-healthy, fills us up, is a great source of fiber, —
and is super-high in vitamin E, helping protect our cells from stress damage

EACH IDEA SERVES 1

We all know popcorn is a delicious snack, but it's often cooked in oil or butter and smothered in lovely caramel and treaty things. That's great—for a treat—but in the spirit of enjoying a super-healthy snack that's also delicious and nutritious, I've tested this really good dry-pan method. I do it all the time now, and the kids love it too! For the best results, I like to cook it just one or two portions at a time.

For a nice portion, like in the picture, put 1 tablespoon of popping corn into a medium non-stick saucepan and place it cold on a medium heat. Starting cold gives you optimum popping conditions. Put a lid on and let it pop, until it stops. As soon as you think it's all popped, turn the heat off—don't overcook it (just avoid eating any kernels that don't pop). If you want to flavor it, apply the flavoring as soon as it's finished popping, shake, and serve—just be careful, as the pan will be super-hot.

WORCESTERSHIRE SAUCE / BALSAMIC VINEGAR FLAVOR

Both of these can really only be successfully distributed if applied with a spritzer (pick one up from a kitchen supply store—you can use it to add flavor to roast veg and meat too). Spritz about fifteen times onto your popcorn, and if choosing vinegar, it's helpful to go for a thin one to help it spritz well.

HOT CHILI SAUCE FLAVOR

Shake 1 teaspoon of hot chili sauce all over your super-hot popcorn. Less is more: too much and it will go soggy, but done at the last minute and shaken well, you'll get stunning results with a nice kick.

MARMITE FLAVOR

Mighty Marmite is particularly good, both in flavor and in the sticky, almost clumpy texture it creates—you'll find 1 teaspoon goes a long way, and I find it easiest to apply from a squeezy bottle.

CALORIES	FAT	SAT FAT	PROTEIN	CARBS	SUGAR	FIBER	
76kcal	0.9g	0.1g	2.6g	14.3g	0.7g	1.5g	15 MINUTES

THESE VALUES ARE AN AVERAGE OF THE FOUR RECIPE IDEAS ABOVE

CUCUMBER STICKS
STUFFED WITH LOVELY THINGS

— We often mistake hunger for thirst, so enjoying refreshing cucumber as a snack is a great idea because it naturally has a really high water content, so will satisfy us on both counts —

EACH SERVES 1

Now this doesn't profess to be cooking—these easy-to-put-together fillings are assembly jobs of staple ingredients that will excite your taste buds. Each stuffed quarter cucumber is under 100 calories, and each recipe uses a whole tub of cream cheese, giving you around 10 portions of filling to keep in the tub, in the fridge, to last a few days.

Halve **1 English cucumber** lengthwise, scrape away the watery core, then halve across the middle. You need one quarter per snack, so wrap and return any extra to the fridge. Sprinkle your cucumber with a little sea salt and **vinegar**.

TAHINI, SCALLION & SESAME

Trim and finely slice **1 scallion**, then mix half with **6 oz of cream cheese**, **2 tablespoons of tahini**, and the **juice of 1 lime**. Spread 1 tablespoon across your **cucumber quarter**, and sprinkle generously with **toasted sesame seeds** and the remaining scallion.

LIME PICKLE & PAPPADAM

Whip **6 oz of cream cheese** with the **juice of ½ a lemon**, then spread 1 tablespoon across your **cucumber quarter**. Spoon over **little blobs of lime or lemon pickle**, then puff up **½ a dry pappadam** per portion for around 30 seconds in the microwave, crunch, and sprinkle over the top like dust.

THE RING OF FIRE

Whip **6 oz of cream cheese** with the **juice of 1 lemon**, put into a sandwich bag, squeeze it into one corner, then snip the bag and pipe splodges along your **cucumber quarter**. Fill the gaps with **Tabasco chipotle sauce**, then slice and sprinkle over some **fresh chile**.

SMOKY PEPPERS & SWEET BASIL

In a blender, blitz **3½ oz of peeled red peppers in brine** (from a jar) with **1 teaspoon of Tabasco chipotle sauce** and the **juice of 1 lemon** until smooth. Loosen **6 oz of cream cheese** with a splash of water, then ripple the pepper mixture through it. Spread 1 tablespoon across your **cucumber quarter** and top with **fresh basil leaves**.

CALORIES	FAT	SAT FAT	PROTEIN	CARBS	SUGAR	FIBER	5 MINUTES
81kcal	6g	0.9g	3.4g	1.9g	1.8g	0.9g	

THESE VALUES ARE AN AVERAGE OF THE FOUR RECIPES ABOVE

BLUSHING PICKLED EGGS
RED CABBAGE, CLOVES & STAR ANISE

— Brilliant eggs are one of the very few foods that are high in the micronutrient iodine, which our thyroid gland needs for making the hormones that help to control our metabolism —

6 large eggs

2 star anise

1 teaspoon cloves

½ tablespoon mustard seeds

2 fresh bay leaves

1 tablespoon liquid honey

1¼ cups red wine vinegar

½ a small red cabbage (10 oz)

This is a slightly bonkers one, I admit, but I love it (my wife would hate it). Making delicious pickled eggs and cabbage is fun, and, most importantly, they can be enjoyed in many ways. First up, one blushing egg makes a great, quick protein-boost snack of just 85 calories, but you could also use the eggs and cabbage to pimp up a picnic, antipasti board, or ploughman's lunch, a salad niçoise, or even a steaming bowl of ramen. This recipe is for 6 eggs, but you can easily double up the ingredients if you want to make a bigger batch.

Gently lower the eggs into a large pan of boiling salted water (a pinch of salt helps to prevent them from bursting). Cook for 10 minutes to hard boil, then place under cold running water. Once cool enough to handle, peel and rinse.

In a large dry casserole pan on a medium heat, toast the star anise, cloves, and mustard seeds until smelling amazing, then add the bay leaves and 1 cup of boiling water. Simmer for 3 minutes, then stir in the honey, vinegar, and 2 heaping teaspoons of sea salt and remove from the heat. Finely shred the red cabbage, then stir it into the pickling liquor and leave for 10 minutes, to let it shrink a little and allow the juices to start exchanging.

Get yourself a 1-liter jar and randomly layer up the cabbage and eggs. Pour in any excess pickling liquor to fill the jar and cover the eggs, then pop the lid on and keep in the fridge until you're ready to tuck in. The eggs are at their most delicious after a week, but perfectly tasty after just 24 hours too. They'll keep happily for 2 weeks, and any leftover liquor is good in salad dressings.

CALORIES	FAT	SAT FAT	PROTEIN	CARBS	SUGAR	FIBER	25 MINUTES PLUS PICKLING
85kcal	6.3g	1.7g	7.2g	0.5g	0.4g	0.1g	

HOMEMADE NUT BUTTERS
FUN, SUPER-TASTY & VERSATILE

___ All nuts are generally packed with a good variety of essential vitamins and minerals, and ___
are a source of unsaturated fat, which is good for keeping our cholesterol happy

MAKES 1 JAR

7 oz of your favorite shelled
   unsalted nuts, such as Brazils,
   almonds, pecans, pistachios,
   hazelnuts, cashews, peanuts

Preheat the oven to 350°F. Lay your chosen nuts or nut combo in a single layer on a baking sheet. Roast for 8 to 10 minutes, or until golden and shiny, then remove and leave to cool for 5 minutes. If you prefer, you can make the nut butter without roasting the nuts first, which gives you a purer color, like the ones at the bottom of this picture. It's still delicious raw, but I find the depth of flavor the roasting brings out is really hard to beat.

Tip the nuts into a food processor or grinder with a small pinch of sea salt—the smaller the receptacle the easier it is to blitz them up. Start blitzing the nuts—they'll quickly go from whole to chopped to finely ground, then they'll take a while longer to turn into nut butter, so be patient and just let the processor do its thing, stopping it occasionally to scrape down the sides and help it along. Blitz to the consistency you like, then decant into a jar.

For a 100-calorie snack, enjoy 1 heaping teaspoon of nut butter with:

+ **3 oz of raw seasonal veg crudités,** such as fennel, carrots, celery, radishes, baby zucchini, asparagus, cucumber, gem lettuce, or heart of romaine

+ **1 dry pappadam,** puffed up in the microwave for around 30 seconds

+ **1 apple or pear,** cut into slices to make a fruit and nut butter kinda sandwich

+ **2 tablespoons of plain yogurt**—swirl them together in a little pot

CALORIES	FAT	SAT FAT	PROTEIN	CARBS	SUGAR	FIBER	
91kcal	5.9g	1.1g	3.1g	6.6g	5.1g	2.1g	25 MINUTES

THESE VALUES ARE BASED ON 1 HEAPING TEASPOON OF NUT BUTTER WITH 80G OF RAW VEG

RAW VEGAN FLAPJACK SNACKS
NUTS, SEEDS, DATES, OATS & FRUIT

These fantastic little pick-me-ups are full of loadsa good stuff, including iron-rich dates—
helping us to stay alert—protein-packed seeds, and a hit of omega 3 from the nuts

MAKES 24

3½ oz unsalted pecans

3½ oz unsalted hazelnuts

¾ oz mixed seeds, such as
    flaxseeds, chia

6 oz Medjool dates

3½ oz mixed unsweetened dried
    berries, such as blueberries,
    cranberries, sour cherries

2 cups rolled oats

2 tablespoons oil (I like
    walnut oil)

1–2 tablespoons maple syrup

Place the nuts, seeds, dates (pit first), and dried fruit in a food processor and briefly blitz until they're all nicely chopped together. Add the oats, oil, and maple syrup and pulse until combined, but still with a bit of texture.

I like to go straight into portion-control mode (my nutrition team will be really proud of me!), and use a 2-inch pastry cutter to portion up the 24 flapjacks there and then. For me, the easiest way to do it without getting the scales out is to scrunch and squash the mixture into a rough 30-inch sausage, simply cut it in half and into quarters, then divide each piece into 6. One by one, pat and push the portions really firmly into the cutter, pushing down in the center and squashing the mixture up the sides with your fingers. As you push it down, remove the cutter to give you a nice round flapjack snack.

Place the snacks in an airtight container, where they'll keep happily for up to 2 weeks. Bag up and freeze any you don't need for a later date. If any get bashed or break up, use them as a great breakfast sprinkle.

CALORIES	FAT	SAT FAT	PROTEIN	CARBS	SUGAR	FIBER	30 MINUTES
100kcal	6.2g	0.5g	2g	10.1g	5.3g	1.7g	

FRO-YO FUN
FRUIT, YOGURT, NUTS & SEEDS

— These fruity fro-yo treats are packed full of good stuff, and having yogurt that contains live bacteria keeps our gut happy. Look out for unsweetened cones to pair it with —

EACH COMBO SERVES 8

RIPE BANANA & BROWN BREAD FRO-YO

In a food processor, blitz **1 lb of frozen peeled banana slices** (it's convenient to chop and freeze your own), **5 oz of crustless whole-grain bread**, and **1 pinch of ground cinnamon** until finely chopped. Add **¾ cup of plain yogurt** and blitz again until smooth.

MANGO, LIME & GINGER FRO-YO

In a food processor, blitz **14 oz of frozen chopped mango, 1 peeled banana, 1½ cups of rolled oats**, the **zest and juice of 1 lime**, and peeled **1¼-inch piece of fresh gingerroot** until finely chopped. Add **¾ cup of plain yogurt** and blitz again until smooth.

BERRY & BROWN BREAD FRO-YO

In a food processor, blitz **14 oz of frozen mixed berries, 1 peeled banana, 5 oz of crustless whole-grain bread**, and the leaves from **2 sprigs of fresh mint** until finely chopped. Add **¾ cup of plain yogurt** and blitz again until smooth.

STRAWBERRY, BALSAMIC & BASIL FRO-YO

In a food processor, blitz **14 oz of frozen chopped strawberries, 1 peeled banana, 1½ cups of rolled oats, 1 tablespoon of balsamic vinegar**, and the leaves from **2 sprigs of fresh basil** until finely chopped. Add **¾ cup of plain yogurt** and blitz again until smooth.

TO SERVE

Serve your fro-yo right away, or you can hold it in a lovely scoopable state in the freezer for up to 40 minutes before it gets too hard. If you want to make it in advance, simply divide between ice-cube trays and freeze completely, then tip those into the food processor and whiz up again when you want to serve. Enjoy in a bowl, a cone, or a wafer, with a sprinkling of toasted nuts and seeds, and some extra fresh fruit to boost your intake.

CALORIES	FAT	SAT FAT	PROTEIN	CARBS	SUGAR	FIBER	5 TO 10 MINUTES
83kcal	1.5g	0.8g	3.2g	14.9g	7.5g	2.3g	

THESE VALUES ARE AN AVERAGE OF THE FOUR RECIPES ABOVE

MY TASTY ENERGY BALLS
DATE, COCOA & PUMPKIN SEED

— Medjool dates have the double benefit of being high in both fiber and chloride, a nutrient that helps our digestion, and we get a hit of copper from the pumpkin seeds —

MAKES 12 PORTIONS

2½ oz raw unsalted pumpkin seeds

1 cup puffed brown rice or puffed quinoa

1¾ oz whole almonds

3 oz Medjool dates

½-inch piece of fresh turmeric or ½ teaspoon ground turmeric

½ teaspoon ground cinnamon

1 heaping teaspoon quality cocoa powder

1 teaspoon vanilla extract

½ tablespoon manuka honey

1 orange

Me and my nutrition team have worked hard to create these super-nutritious, balanced, flavor-packed balls that give us the perfect snack boost to get us through the day—enjoy two balls per snack.

Blitz 1½ oz of the pumpkin seeds into a fine dust in a food processor, then decant onto a plate. Place the remaining pumpkin seeds and the puffed rice or quinoa in the processor with the almonds and dates (pit first), then blitz until finely chopped. Peel and finely grate in the turmeric, if using fresh, or add the ground turmeric, along with the cinnamon, cocoa powder, and a pinch of sea salt. Blitz again until finely ground, then add the vanilla, honey, and half the orange juice. Blitz for another 1 to 2 minutes, stopping to scrape down the sides a couple of times, and adding an extra squeeze of orange juice to bind, only if needed—it takes a while for the mixture to come together, so be patient and let the processor work its magic.

With wet hands, divide into 24 and roll into balls, dropping them into the pumpkin seed dust as you go. Shake to coat, storing them in the excess dust until needed. They'll keep happily for up to 2 weeks in an airtight container.

CALORIES	FAT	SAT FAT	PROTEIN	CARBS	SUGAR	FIBER	25 MINUTES
80kcal	5.2g	0.6g	2.7g	6g	4.2g	0.5g	

MY TASTY ENERGY BALLS
APRICOT, GINGER & CASHEW

_ Dried apricots are a brilliant veggie-friendly source of iron and are super-high
in potassium, a mineral that our muscles need in order to function properly _

MAKES 12 PORTIONS

3½ oz unsalted cashews

¾ oz raw sesame seeds

3 oz dried apricots

1 cup puffed brown rice or puffed
quinoa

1½-inch piece of fresh gingerroot

½ teaspoon pumpkin pie spice

2 tablespoons manuka honey

Me and my nutrition team have worked hard to create these super-nutritious, balanced, flavor-packed balls that give us the perfect snack boost to get us through the day—enjoy two balls per snack. Toast the cashews and sesame seeds in a dry non-stick pan on a medium heat until lightly golden, tossing occasionally, then tip onto a plate and leave to cool.

Remove 1½ oz of the cashews and blitz into a fine dust in a food processor, then decant onto a separate plate. Place the remaining cashews and sesame seeds, the apricots, and puffed rice or quinoa in the processor and blitz until finely chopped. Peel and finely grate in the ginger, and add the pumpkin pie spice. Blitz again until finely ground, then add the honey. Blitz for another 1 to 2 minutes, stopping to scrape down the sides a couple of times, and adding an extra squeeze of honey to bind, only if needed—it takes a while for the mixture to come together, so be patient and let the processor work its magic.

With wet hands, divide into 24 and roll into balls, dropping them into the ground cashew dust as you go. Shake to coat, storing them in the excess dust until needed. They'll keep happily for up to 2 weeks in an airtight container.

CALORIES	FAT	SAT FAT	PROTEIN	CARBS	SUGAR	FIBER	
86kcal	5.1g	1g	2.4g	8.2g	6.2g	0.9g	25 MINUTES

1.

2.

3.

5.

6.

7.

9.

10.

11.

13.

14.

15.

SNACK ATTACK

It's good to have a quick nibble when feeling hungry to keep our energy and focus up, and all these nuts, seeds, and dried fruits have lots of lovely nutritional benefits. So—as simple as it may be—each pile on this page shows us roughly what 100 calories really looks like. I hope it will empower you to be a bit more conscious about the amount you're snacking on, and inspire you to mix things up. Just remember to keep an eye on your portion control!

1.   1¼ oz raisins

2.   10 unsalted cashew nuts

3.   3 or 4 dried figs

4.   8 unsalted macadamia nuts

5.   ½ oz raw unsalted sunflower seeds

6.   1 oz dried unsweetened cranberries

7.   ½ oz shelled unsalted pistachio nuts

8.   7 unsalted pecan nuts

9.   ½ oz unsalted hazelnuts

10.   15 unsalted whole almonds

11.   1¼ oz dried unsweetened blueberries

12.   ½ oz raw unsalted pumpkin seeds

13.   4 unsalted Brazil nuts

14.   7 dried apricots

15.   4 shelled unsalted walnut halves

16.   1¼ oz sultanas

EASY FLAVORED WATERS

CUCUMBER, APPLE & MINT

Finely slice **1 apple**, ideally on a mandolin (use the guard!). Peel strips of **cucumber** lengthwise, then add both to a pitcher of water over ice. Pick in some **fresh mint leaves**, and stir to get the party started.

ST. CLEMENTS

Simply slice up **lemons, oranges**, and, if you're lucky enough for them to be in season, **blood oranges**, and add to a pitcher of water over ice. A few **fresh mint or lemon balm leaves** are also delicious.

COLORFUL, BRIGHT & DELICIOUS

WATERMELON & BASIL

Peel and clank up a **wedge of watermelon** and add to a pitcher of water with lots of ice, then pick in some **fresh basil leaves**. Stir and bash up the watermelon to get the flavors going. Nice with a squeeze of **lime juice**.

POMEGRANATE, GINGER & LIME

Hold half a **pomegranate** cut-side down in your fingers and bash the back with a spoon so the seeds tumble into your pitcher. Finely grate in some **ginger**, slice and add **1 lime** and a **load of ice**, then top up with water.

THERAPEUTIC TEAS

FENNEL SEEDS, LEMON & HONEY

Slice **1 lemon** and place in a teapot with **1 teaspoon of fennel seeds**. Stir in 1 liter of just-boiling water, steep for 5 minutes, then strain through a sieve and enjoy hot, sweetening to taste with **liquid honey**.

GRAPEFRUIT, ORANGE & MINT

Slice ½ **a grapefruit** (pink if you can get it) and **1 orange** and place in a teapot with **a few sprigs of fresh mint**. Stir in 1 liter of just-boiling water, steep for 5 minutes, and enjoy hot, or cool to enjoy as iced tea.

TASTY, VIBRANT & EASY

GINGER, TURMERIC, LEMON & HONEY

Slice **a piece of ginger** and place in a teapot with ¼ of a teaspoon of ground turmeric and 1 sliced lemon. Stir in 1 liter of just-boiling water, steep for 5 minutes, and enjoy hot, sweetening to taste with **liquid honey.**

STRAWBERRY, HIBISCUS & STAR ANISE

Halve **a few strawberries** and place in a teapot with 2 teaspoons of dried hibiscus flowers and 1 star anise. Stir in 1 liter of just-boiling water, steep for 5 minutes, strain, and enjoy hot, or cool to enjoy as iced tea.

LIVE WELL

A HEALTHIER, HAPPIER YOU

While working on this book I've been reading up on nutrition, I've been studying for a nutrition diploma, and I've had the privilege of meeting lots of incredible scientists, professors, and experts in their field so that I can share the most useful and accessible info that's out there with you. And it's been the most incredibly inspiring journey, seeing food and lifestyle from a totally different perspective.

So in the pages that follow, I'm going to share what I've learnt around some key areas within health, nutrition, and well-being. I hope you'll find this information as fascinating as I do, and remember—you really can make positive, sustainable change just by doing the odd thing differently, building on small new habits. I've taken into account everything I talk about in these pages in the development of each and every recipe in the book, so if you just pick up your shopping and get cooking, you'll be in a beautiful place. Happy days.

MY PHILOSOPHY IN THIS BOOK
THE BALANCED PLATE

We all know that balance is absolutely key—but what does it really mean? This page exists to make that super-clear, because if you can get your balanced plate right and keep your portion control in check—which I've done for you with all the recipes in this book—you can be confident that you're giving yourself a really great start on the path to good health.

One of the most useful things you can remember is that you don't have to be spot-on every day—just try to get your balance right across the week. Mix up your choices within the chapters to ensure you're having a varied diet and a wide range of nutrients, and you'll be getting everything you need. As a general guide for main meals, if you eat meat and fish, you're looking at at least two portions of fish a week, one of which should be oily (such as salmon, trout, or mackerel), then splitting the rest of the week's main meals between brilliant meat-free plant-based meals, some poultry, and a little red meat. An all-vegetarian diet can be perfectly healthy too.

WHAT IS THE BALANCED PLATE?

Bear with me on this one—it's going to get a little technical—but it's important to register the facts up front about how to approach putting a meal together. Just look at the table below and you'll get the gist—it's easy really.

THE FIVE FOOD GROUPS (UK)	PROPORTION OF YOUR BALANCED PLATE
Vegetables and fruit	One-third of your plate
Starchy carbohydrates (bread, rice, potatoes, pasta)	One-third of your plate
Protein (meat, fish, eggs, beans, other non-dairy sources)	Around one-sixth of your plate
Dairy foods and milk	Around one-sixth of your plate
Fat/sugar-high foods	Try to only eat a small amount of food high in fat and/or sugar

HOW DOES THAT WORK IN THIS BOOK?

Working closely with my lovely nutrition team and following UK guidelines, I've structured all the recipes in a really clear and easy-to-follow way:

+ All the breakfast recipes are less than 400 calories per portion and contain less than 4g of saturated fat and less than 1.5g of salt

+ All the lunches and dinners are less than 600 calories per portion and contain less than 6g of saturated fat and less than 1.5g of salt—so all of these recipes are interchangeable across the two chapters

I've also included snacks of up to 100 calories, giving you the freedom to enjoy a few tasty energy-boosting snacks a day, with some calories left for drinks.

WHAT DOES THAT MEAN IN REAL LIFE?

In general, the average woman needs about 2,000 calories a day, while the average man can have about 2,500. I'm sure you're aware that these figures are just a guide, and what we eat always needs to be considered in relation to factors like age, build, lifestyle, and activity levels. The good news is that all food and drinks can be eaten and drunk in moderation as part of a healthy, balanced diet, so we don't have to completely give up anything that we really enjoy, unless we're advised to do so by a doctor or dietitian.

My grandad's philosophy on life was simple—everything in moderation and a little bit of what you like—and that still stands very true today. Even nutritionists eat cake!

BRILLIANT BEAUTIFUL BREAKFAST

Here's one super-easy thing that I want you to take from this book: eat breakfast! Simple as that. This mighty meal is often overlooked, but it's so important in setting you up for the day. Not only will it fill you up and help prevent you snacking on foods high in fat/sugar, it can kick you off with a boost of micronutrients, such as iron, fiber, the B vitamins, and vitamin D. It's been shown that when you miss breakfast you're unlikely to make up on those missed nutrients throughout the rest of the day, so get into good habits and build it into your daily routine from the outset.

CELEBRATING H_2O

Drinking water is absolutely essential. Although it's not—for obvious reasons—part of the balanced plate, it is totally integral to a balanced diet. It keeps us hydrated and alert, and keeps our bodies functioning properly. Often when we think we're hungry we're actually dehydrated, so drinking plenty of water can also help prevent us over-eating! Like anything, our requirements vary depending on factors such as age, gender, build, lifestyle, and activity levels, as well as things like humidity and the temperature around us. As a general rule, women should aim for at least 6¾ cups per day, while men need at least 8 cups. Embrace it, celebrate it, and enjoy humble H_2O every day. Read more about the wonderful world of hydration on page 278.

ILLUSTRIOUS VEG & FRUIT

To live a good, healthy life, veg and fruit need to be right at the heart of your diet. The wide bounty of incredible vitamins and minerals we get from the array of veg and fruit out there is honestly astounding.

And by the way, you'll notice I'm referring to veg and fruit, not fruit and veg. It's a great philosophy I picked up from Professor Julie Lovegrove about how we should think about our natural friends: fruit is brilliantly nutritious and we should definitely embrace it, but veggies shouldn't be thought of as second best. Veg and fruit are at the core of the best diets in the world, and why all the recipes in this book are so colorful, vibrant, and exciting.

EAT THE RAINBOW

Veg and fruit come in all kinds of shapes, sizes, colors, flavors, and textures, and help us to navigate the seasons in a wonderful way. There's no denying their nutrient value, so the best thing we can do to take advantage of this nutritious bounty is to eat the rainbow, enjoying as wide a variety as possible.

HOW MUCH SHOULD WE EAT?

We've all heard about 5-a-day, but I'm here to tell you that we should all be aiming for at least 5-a-day, ideally more. I think five is a compromise because here in the UK we're not doing too well on our consumption, so this lower target dumbs down our expectations. The reality is we should be trying to get seven or eight portions a day. Look at other countries with higher targets— Australia advocates five veg and two fruit portions every day! Plant-based diets are also more prevalent in many of the communities around the world with the highest proportion of centenarians (see page 292).

THE KNOWN HEALTH BENEFITS

Things we know for sure about these nutritional powerhouses are that veg and fruit can help us maintain a healthy weight and a healthy heart, as well as reducing the risk of strokes and some cancers. They are also packed with dietary fiber, keeping us regular (which is a good thing!) and helping reduce the risk of strokes and some cancers. They really should be embraced at every meal, and they make great snacks, too.

THE UNKNOWN HEALTH BENEFITS

The brilliant thing about veg and fruit is that there's loads of hidden stuff we're yet to uncover too. For example, I can tell you that broccoli is high in folic acid and vitamin C, but nutritionists are looking at lots of other stuff on top of that, more nutrients, vitamins, minerals, and trace elements that are beneficial to the body in many, many ways. Sounds pretty amazing, right—veg and fruit is where it's at! And this is why it's so important to eat the rainbow to get maximum goodness.

+ 3 oz of fresh, frozen, or tinned veg or fruit is considered a portion—that's what I've worked to in the recipes in this book. Because we should be eating a wide variety of veg and fruit, we can only count each variety as one portion, so even if you eat 5½ oz of carrots, for example, it would still only count as one portion of your 5-a-day

+ 1 oz of dried fruit is considered a portion. I only count one portion a day. Dried fruit is natural, but the sugar is more concentrated

+ ⅔ cup of unsweetened veg or fruit juice can be counted as one portion only each day. A lot of nutrients and fiber are lost when veg and fruit are juiced, which is why it only counts as one of your 5-a-day—personally, I don't count juice at all in my tally. Smoothies are a better choice

+ 3 oz of beans or pulses—about 3 big tablespoons—can be counted as one portion only each day, and also give us protein

+ And for all you spud lovers out there, I have to point out that our humble potatoes don't count towards our 5-a-day as they're a starchy food so go into our carb tally instead (see page 266). Non-starchy sweet potatoes, on the other hand, do count

GROWING YOUR OWN

In the areas of the world where people live the longest, many of them grow their own food. If you've never tried, I recommend giving it a go. It's the best hobby—it'll keep you fit and save you cash; your relationship with planet earth will become more meaningful (I challenge anyone not to be inspired by watching stuff grow); and best of all, you get to eat the veg, and fruits, of your labor! Plus, if you've got kids, it will get them engaged in food in the most fun, dynamic way. You don't need a garden or a field to get involved—a window box, flat roof, allotment, balcony, pot, grow-bag, or bucket all work fine—I've even grown stuff in a gutter pipe!

KEEPING IT FRESH

When you pick stuff straight from the ground it's at its freshest and most nutritious. I get a geeky buzz about turning something into a meal that's been in the ground just minutes before. If you've got a farmer's market nearby and you know stuff's been picked that morning, take advantage of it. As soon as veg are picked, their nutrient levels start to deplete, so eating them as fresh as possible—even raw, if you like—is going to give you more goodness per mouthful.

SHOULD WE GO ORGANIC?

Buying local, seasonal, organic produce is always going to be optimal for our health (read more on page 284).

In the Nicoya Peninsula, Costa Rica, I met a community of some of the oldest people on the planet. They cite the humongous amount of fruit they eat as one of their secrets to longevity. But, variety is key. Many of us eat the same type of fruit, week in, week out, but each fruit contains a different cocktail of vitamins, minerals, and elements our bodies love and need, so to get the most benefit, mixing up our choices is crucial.

CELEBRATING GOOD CARBOHYDRATES

Starchy carbohydrates are a wonderful thing—they make us feel happy, satisfied, and energetic, and quite simply, we need carbohydrates in our diet as they provide a large proportion of the energy we need to move our bodies, and the fuel our organs need to function.

Plus, we all crave and enjoy them. This page exists to help you understand what carbohydrates are, which ones we should be eating, and to dispel all those myths that are giving carbs a bad name. If you know how carbohydrates both work within and affect our bodies, and just why we need them, you can have a much healthier attitude towards them and not buy into a faddy no-carb diet that I'm sure you'll end up crashing out of.

WHAT ARE CARBOHYDRATES?

It's important to recognize that not all carbs are equal—this is where I think the confusion lies. Carbohydrates are either sugars, starch that will eventually be broken down into glucose (a form of sugar) in the gut, or dietary fiber, which we can't break down. So, it's the type and how we consume it that has most impact.

Let me break it down how I see it. Foods that are rich in carbs fall into four main categories:

+ Simple sugars—white and brown sugar, honey, maple syrup

+ White complex carbohydrates—bread, pasta, rice, flour, cereal

+ Whole-grain and whole-wheat complex carbo-hydrates—bread, pasta, rice, flour, cereal

+ Vegetables and fruit—root veg in particular, such as carrots, sweet potatoes, rutabaga, turnips, parsnips

WHAT CARBS SHOULD WE BE EATING?

Simple carbs, such as white refined sugar or sugary processed foods and drinks, can be digested really quickly and are empty calories, giving us a blood sugar spike followed by an energy low that can leave us feeling sluggish. Eating more complex carbohydrates is key—they take longer to break down, are slow-releasing, and give us a more sustained level of energy. Even better, choose whole-grain and whole-wheat varieties, as these also contain more fiber and other nutrients that our bodies can use and take even longer to digest, helping to keep us feeling fuller for longer. I tend to trade up to whole-grain and whole-wheat at least 7 times out of 10—not only are you upping the nutritional value of what you're eating, you're also getting some really delicious flavors and textures, and that drip-feed of energy is more useful. While veg and fruit are often rich in carbs too, because they have such high nutrient values they go into our veg and fruit tally instead (see page 262).

WHY DO CARBS HAVE A BAD REP?

So when people are criticizing carbs, it's generally our excessive sweet tooth that's the problem. It's a huge sweeping statement to say that carbs make us fat. Obviously, like anything, if we consume more than we need, that excess is going to be stored as fat in the body, but if we eat the right type of carbs, we should all be in a happy place. I'm sure you're aware that many sugary foods also tend to be high in saturated fat, often don't contain any other useful nutrients, and can have a very detrimental effect on our health if consumed too often.

WHY DO WE NEED CARBS?

If we don't get enough carbohydrates and our bodies don't get the energy they need, they have to get it from elsewhere and break down fat and protein instead. Protein (see page 268) is essential to the growth and repair of our bodies, so using it up for energy is inefficient and could eventually lead to muscle wastage. Eating complex carbohydrates is the best way to maintain our blood sugar levels, which helps us to concentrate and carry out our daily chores. So forget that fear of carbs and include them in your diet in the right way, every day.

WHY I LOVE CARBS

Let's just pause from the science for a minute to acknowledge what an integral part of the wonderful world of ingredients carbohydrates are. They are some of the most incredible flavor carriers on the planet—pasta paired with insane sauces, delicious breads and grains, rice in all its guises (stir-fries, risottos, paellas, with curries, stews, in soups), noodles, I could go on . . .

HOW MUCH CAN WE EAT?

What I will say is, because these complex carbohydrates come in so many wonderful different shapes and forms, it can be easy to double up and have too much without realizing, so portion control and, frankly, restraint—AKA four roast potatoes, not nine—is the name of the game. Carbs should be about one-third of your balanced plate, and ultimately it's what you pair those with that'll get you on or off the right track. The average adult can have around 260g of carbohydrates a day, with up to 90g coming from total sugars.

FANTASTIC FIBER

Fiber is also classed as a carbohydrate, and is found mainly in plant-based foods. We should be aiming for about 30g of fiber each day—I've included it in the nutrition box on the recipe pages so you can start to get an idea of how much you get from different meals. We consume two different types:

+ Insoluble fiber—largely found in whole-grain and whole-wheat foods. We can't digest this, so its important function is to help other food and waste pass through the gut, keeping our insides happy

+ Soluble fiber—found in foods such as amazing oats, pulses, beans, veg, and fruit. We can't digest this, but the good bugs in our colon can, which keeps them happy. Also, oats have a proven health claim to reduce blood cholesterol, so we love, love, love them

THE POWER OF PROTEIN

So let's talk about protein. First up, as a chef I must say the word "protein" is kind of annoying, as the term doesn't give any romance to all the incredible plants, legumes, and animals it refers to.

At the same time, there are a lot of misconceptions around protein and its benefits, with some fad diets hailing it as the answer to everything. While protein is definitely an integral part of our diet, it does—like everything else—need to be eaten in the right amounts. I'm going to focus here on what protein does, what it actually is, how much we need, and what my beliefs around welfare and standards are when it comes to different protein sources.

WHAT DOES PROTEIN DO?

Protein is mighty—think of it as the building blocks of our bodies. It is absolutely essential for the growth and repair of muscle tissue, as well as building hormones, enzymes that build and break down substances in our bodies, and antibodies in our immune systems. This list, as I'm sure you'll recognize, is basically everything that's important to how we grow, repair, feel, break down, and absorb things, and how we fight disease and infections. Whether you're a seasoned carnivore, a pescatarian, a veggie, or a vegan, protein really is your best friend and should be enjoyed in the right way.

WHAT IS PROTEIN?

I think it's important for me not to get too technical here, but basically, proteins are made up of a cocktail of 20 different amino acids. A lot are made in our body, but we have to get the rest from the food we eat.

Just like carbohydrates (see page 266), not all protein sources are equal. Let me break it down:

+ Complete proteins—meat, fish, eggs, milk, cheese

+ Incomplete proteins—beans, nuts, seeds, lentils, cereals, quinoa, oats, peas, tofu, bread, flour, corn

That's not to say that the complete sources are superior, they're just different—think of them as a one-stop shop. What's important is to eat a wide range of different proteins across the week, and that way you've got a really good chance of getting it right. You might have also heard the term "complementary proteins." This refers to mixing up your incomplete protein sources with each other in order to build up your volume of amino acids—baked beans on toast or rice and peas are perfect examples of this, and as well as being a match made in heaven on the taste front, are great combos to give you a high amino acid level.

HOW MUCH PROTEIN DO WE NEED?

Generally, the optimal amount of protein to aim for is 45g a day for women aged 19–50 (which varies with factors such as pregnancy and breast-feeding), and 55g a day for men in the same age bracket. In the UK we usually get enough, but we do need to be mindful that we're not having too much. About one-sixth of our balanced plate should be made up of protein.

Your balance across a week in terms of meat and fish consumption should generally be at least two portions of fish, one of which should be oily (such as salmon, trout, or mackerel), then you want to split the rest of the week between meat-free, poultry, and a little red meat.

Some diets advocate high protein consumption, particularly for weight control or building muscle mass, but this can have a whole cascade of negative effects, especially if combined with low carb intake. If you're not an athlete, nor have been advised by a doctor to up your protein levels, excessive consumption isn't a good idea—it can increase our risk of osteoporosis, too much red meat increases the risk of bowel cancer, and we can only metabolize a certain amount of protein anyway, so we excrete the excess through our urine.

WELFARE, STANDARDS & PROVENANCE

For me, there's no point in eating meat unless it's been raised well and the animal was at optimal health. Choosing grass-fed animals where possible, that are free to roam and haven't lived in a stressful environment is essential—it makes total sense to me that what we put into our bodies should have lived a good life, to in turn give us goodness. It's about quality over quantity, so please choose organic, free-range, or higher-welfare meat and responsibly sourced fish whenever you can.

I'm aware—as journalists often mention—that it does cost more to trade up. This isn't because anyone's being ripped off, but normally because the animal has lived a better-quality, longer life. Remember that you can trade up to higher-welfare meat and still buy the cheaper cuts, such as chicken thighs and minced meat. With clever buying skills and a slight reduction in your overall meat consumption, which is no bad thing, you can afford to improve on quality—double the pleasure.

I feel even more passionate about organic or free-range eggs, and organic milk, yogurt, and butter—the trade-up cost is less, the welfare comparisons are dramatic, and we use them a lot, so it makes sense (see page 274).

VEGGIE & VEGAN DIETS

Interestingly, these are looking really rather successful in health terms. Although meat and fish proteins are complete and robust in so many micronutrients, following a vegetarian or vegan diet just means you have to be a bit cleverer about your protein sources. Brilliant veggie options kick off with black beans, the highest source of bean protein, plus all the other beans, pulses, legumes, lentils, tofu, quinoa, and chia. Vitamin B12, which is prolific in meat, can often be deficient in vegans. We need it to aid growth, for good digestion, to keep our nerves healthy, produce energy, and maintain healthy blood cells. You can get it through supplements if you want, or by eating some forms of algae, so maybe supplements are looking good!

In Ikaria, Greece—which I'm told has more 90-year-olds than anywhere else on the planet—I learnt how to make trahana, a cracked whole-wheat and goat's-milk mixture, with the lovely Maria. Embracing grains and choosing whole-grain and whole-wheat foods is one really simple, positive change we can all make. Not only do they taste amazing and have great texture, they're full of fiber, which can lower cholesterol, helping to prevent heart disease. High-fiber foods also help to keep our bowels healthy and keep us feeling fuller for longer.

FAT IS ESSENTIAL

Let's bust a myth right off—there's no need to be afraid of fat, it's not the enemy it's been portrayed as.

Of course, our fat consumption needs to be controlled—at 9 calories per gram it's the nutrient with the highest caloric value, but just because you eat fat doesn't mean you'll get fat. Fat is found naturally in our bodies, and some fats we can only get from the food we eat, so it is an essential part of our diet—without it, we'll die.

WHY DO WE NEED FAT?

Its main role is to provide energy, and fat is the way we store excess food energy. This is what allows us to draw on our reserves when food is in short supply—think of it as our natural battery. Adding fat to a meal is the most effective way of increasing the energy content—we also get energy from carbohydrates (see page 266). What's worth remembering is that if we are massively over-consuming fat, and our body doesn't need that much, we will put on weight as our stores build up.

WHAT DOES FAT DO?

Fat provides insulation and protection to our internal organs, and a certain amount of body fat is needed to support fertility for all you ladies out there. What's really crucial is that it supplies some fat-soluble vitamins and essential fatty acids, such as omega-3 and -6. In our weird and wonderful bodies many nutrients need the presence of fat to be properly absorbed. For example, having a little oil-based salad dressing is better than no dressing at all—it means we're able to absorb more vitamin A, in the form of beta-carotene, from the veg.

TYPES OF FAT

+ Unsaturated fats—these are generally the healthier type of fats to consume, where the dominant fatty acid is either monounsaturated or polyunsaturated. They're found in olive oil and other liquid vegetable oils (see right), as well as nuts, legumes, avocados, and omega-3-rich oily fish. Some oils help lower bad cholesterol and raise the good stuff—we like that

+ Saturated fats—animal fats (butter, lard, suet, meat fat) tend to contain more saturated fatty acids, but also contain monounsaturated fatty acids. These fats are usually solid at room temperature. Because saturated fats raise cholesterol levels, we should be mindful of our consumption of them. They have also been linked with an increased risk of heart disease

HOW MUCH FAT DO WE NEED?

All fats should be eaten in moderation. In the UK, it's recommended that the average woman gets no more than 70g of fat per day, with less than 20g of that from saturated fat, and the average man no more than 90g a day, with less than 30g coming from saturates.

THE HEALTHIEST OILS

One of the easiest ways to get good fats into your diet is to use a little oil in your cooking. Keep a range in your pantry for different purposes. Here's my top five:

+ Olive & extra virgin olive oil—super-high in omega-9, use cheaper, lighter olive oil for lower-temperature cooking, and save extra virgin olive oil for dressings and finishing. Worth a special mention is cold-pressed new season's extra virgin olive oil—if you can get your hands on some each year, and only use it over that year while it's at its best, you'll be very happy

+ Rapeseed oil—a good source of omega-3, -6, and vitamin E, this contains half the saturated fat of olive oil. It has a fairly neutral flavor, so is great in all sorts of dishes and probably the most affordable healthy oil option out there. Look for cold-pressed varieties

+ Walnut oil—a good source of omega-3 and -6, this oil is brilliant for dressings, marinades, and finishing and can be used to great effect in baking

+ Avocado oil—with the natural goodness of avocados, this is super-high in monounsaturated fats, omega-9, and vitamin E, and is useful for lower-temperature cooking, dressings, marinades, and finishing

+ Sunflower oil—an excellent source of omega-6 and vitamin E, this is a great, cheap oil to have in stock for higher-temperature cooking

Other oils I use are omega-3-rich hemp oil, omega-9-rich almond oil, peanut or vegetable oil for higher-temperature cooking, and sesame oil for Asian-style cooking, dressings, and marinades.

OMEGA FATTY ACIDS

We need omega-6 fatty acids for many functions, including growth and development, and to maintain healthy skin—we generally get plenty of these in the diet. Omega-3 fatty acids are needed in smaller amounts to help keep our brains and hearts in tip-top condition, as well as to help to reduce our risk of heart attacks and strokes. Omega-3 sources are more limited—oily fish and vegetable oils are our best bet. Both of these essential polyunsaturated fatty acids can't be made in the body, so we have to get them from food. We can, however, make omega-9 fatty acids in the body, but it's still beneficial to use oils rich in them rather than saturated fats to help lower cholesterol and prevent heart attacks.

THE COCONUT OIL MYTH

There are so many health gurus shouting about the health benefits of coconut oil, so I spoke to the leading fat specialist in the UK, Professor Tom Sanders, and others, and they all have the same opinion on this. Now I'm not anti coconut oil, but I am anti its overuse and the fictitious benefits being bandied around it. It's absorbed and turned into energy more quickly, which is perceived as helpful, but it's still the highest saturated fat on the planet and very low in essential fatty acids. If you consume too much, it will nudge you in the direction of heart disease. My advice is to use it in moderation and only in dishes where it adds appropriate flavor, such as curries.

DIPPING INTO DAIRY

Dairy is a really interesting food group. Global nutritionists have given it its own slice of the balanced plate because it offers an amazing array of nutrients and is a really good natural food source.

So—unless you're a vegan—this is a lovely area. Milk, yogurt, cheese, butter, cream—sounds good to me. Though of course it's worth remembering that it's milk, yogurt, and small amounts of cheese we should be favoring as the portion of dairy in our meals—butter and cream are very high in fat and saturated fat and don't provide the full package of nutrients milk, yogurt, and cheese give us, so butter and cream don't count towards our dairy portion.

WHAT IS DAIRY?

Produced primarily by cows, dairy products can also come from sheep, goats, and even buffalo. Being just a small part of the balanced plate, around one-sixth of our meals should be made up of dairy.

EASY DAIRY CHOICES

Embracing the balanced-plate philosophy, you'll find a little bit of dairy in the majority of meals in this book. The easiest way to add dairy is to serve your meals with a dollop of yogurt or a little bit of cheese. As well as Parmesan and ricotta, you'll see me using a lot of feta and cottage cheese because not only are they great carriers of flavor, but they can be used in really diverse ways and are much lower in fat than most other cheeses. If you've got a meal that doesn't contain dairy, why not have a little glass of milk with or after it to supplement it, or have some yogurt and fruit as a snack to get your balance back on track.

WHY DO WE NEED DAIRY?

It contains key nutrients to keep us strong and healthy:

+ Protein—crucial for growth and repair

+ Calcium—for strong bones and healthy teeth (especially during childhood and our teenage years, while our bones are still growing and developing)

+ Vitamin A—for good eye health (this is only found in dairy products that also contain fat)

+ Riboflavin—for healthy skin and helping us digest carbs (milk is the main source in our diets)

+ Iodine—helps to regulate our metabolism so our thyroid gland can function efficiently

In order to efficiently absorb calcium from the food we eat, we need vitamin D—we get this naturally from sunlight, and can top up with oily fish and eggs, or even mushrooms that have been left near a window to soak up a couple of hours of sunshine (believe me!).

TRADING UP TO ORGANIC

With those dairy products that we use as staple ingredients—milk, yogurt, butter—I honestly couldn't endorse more the trade up to organic. It is slightly more expensive, but not vastly so, and every time you buy organic you vote for a better food system (see page 284). In the EU, organic means that the cows have grazed on grass free from chemical fertilizers, pesticides, and agrochemicals. They won't have been routinely fed antibiotics, and will have lived a better life with the best welfare standards, meaning they live an average of two years longer! I like the sound of that. It's better for the environment, too. In some parts of the world, non-organic cows may never even get to step onto grass and are kept indoors within "mega-dairies." Sad but true.

DAIRY INTOLERANCE

Here in the UK, around 3% of people have a food allergy or intolerance, and dairy intolerance has become more common in recent years. It's caused when our bodies lack an enzyme called lactase, which breaks down the natural sugar found in dairy foods. An intolerance to a certain type of protein found in cow's milk also exists. If you think you have an intolerance, chat to your GP or a dietitian. As we get better at diagnosis, the number of dairy alternatives in the shops is rising. Even if you're not lactose intolerant, it's nice to mix up your choices to take advantage of the different flavors on offer (see right)—this is something we do in the Oliver household.

MILK IS INCREDIBLE

It has a super-high nutrient density for most of the key nutrients and, in the grand scheme of things, is pretty low in fat. Milk is actually better at hydrating the body than water or sports drinks after exercise.

TYPES OF DAIRY MILK

+ Cow's milk—whether you enjoy whole, semi-skimmed, or skimmed is down to personal preference. All are great choices nutrient-wise, but the calorie and sat fat levels are higher in whole, so watch your consumption

+ Goat's milk—it tastes a little funkier than cow's milk and has similar lactose levels, but the fat globules are typically smaller, so are easier for us to digest

ALTERNATIVES TO DAIRY MILK

Most alternative milks are fortified with calcium, B vitamins (including B12, which we can't get from plant-based foods), and vitamins D2 and E, to mirror the benefits of dairy milk. All those listed here are good for veggies and vegans, too. Choose unsweetened, when you can.

+ Organic soya milk—high in protein and low in sat fat, plus widely available, this is great for all-round use

+ Almond milk—subtly nutty and light in texture, this is great for breakfasts, such as pancakes, oatmeal, and smoothies. It's low in fat, sat fat, and sugar

+ Hazelnut milk—with a wonderful nutty flavor, this is perfect for smoothies and even baking

+ Oat milk—great for breakfast recipes and naturally low in fat and sat fat, mighty oats are proven to lower blood cholesterol if consumed regularly

Here, I'm out collecting seaweed with Tadashi in Okinawa, Japan, where some of the oldest people on the planet live. I was amazed to learn that seaweed is the most nutritious plant there is—that's crazy! And many people I met in Japan swear that it's one of the things that has kept them going so long. So wherever you are in the world, seaweed is definitely one to look out for. It has more vitamins, minerals, and proteins than any vegetable that grows in the soil, is packed with B vitamins, iodine, antioxidants, fatty acids, calcium, and fiber—you can't argue with that. You can already pick up dried seaweed pretty easily—simply rehydrate, shred, and add to salads or stir-fries.

DRINK WATER & THRIVE

If you want to be the very best you can be, staying hydrated is absolutely key. This section is naturally a celebration of one of the most important, calorie-free, life-giving substances on the planet—H_2O.

Most of us are aware of how important it is to stay hydrated—I'm sure it's been drummed into us since we were kids. You might even have been subjected to one of those graded-color wee charts in the toilet, which in our youth I'm sure we all found funny, but all joking aside, they're actually really useful and this is a serious subject.

WHY IS IT SO IMPORTANT?

It wasn't until I sat down earlier this year, during my nutrition diploma, for a hydration lesson, that I really understood just how integral water is to pretty much every function of the human body. Let's not forget, nearly two-thirds of our body is made up of water! If we're dehydrated, our bodies and brains won't function in the optimal way. This could be how we feel, heal, or react, our ability to absorb nutrients from the food we eat, or the way our cells and organs function—dehydration really does affect everything we do. Also, our bodies often mistake hunger for thirst, so making sure we keep hydrated throughout the day can help to prevent us from over-eating and consuming calories we don't need. Water is a cheap, obvious, accessible part of the diet that has an immediate and dramatic impact on the way we function and feel. If you take just a handful of things from this book, bigging up H_2O and staying hydrated is one of the most valuable actions you can build into your daily habits.

WHY DO WE FEEL THIRSTY?

As wonderful as the human body is, there is a bit of a lag between our bodies telling our brains that we're actually thirsty and our brains communicating that message. So if you're feeling thirsty, a) you are definitely dehydrated, and b) you were probably dehydrated an hour ago. If you're a parent, it's worth noting that kids are even worse at recognizing when they're thirsty, so it's important to keep reminding them to drink water.

HOW MUCH FLUID DO WE NEED?

The average woman should be getting at least 6¾ cups a day, while the average man is looking at at least 8 cups a day. Like anything, these amounts are a guideline, and our requirements vary depending on factors such as age, build, lifestyle, and activity levels, as well as humidity and the temperature around us. Teas and herbal teas, coffee, fruit juice, and milk all contribute to our hydration. It's thought that we also get about 20% of our water intake from the food we eat, such as veggies and fruit with a high water content.

KEEP WATER HANDY

My top tip, as ridiculously obvious as it sounds, is to put it in front of you! If you've always got water at hand—a glass at your desk, a pitcher on the kitchen table, a bottle when you're out and about—you're more likely to pick it up and drink it throughout the day. If you want to naturally flavor it sometimes to keep things interesting, check out the easy ideas on page 254.

TASTY TAP WATER

British tap water goes through loads of checks, so it's safe, clean, and should definitely be utilized. It does change in taste regionally—and I know in some places you can taste chlorine—but it's there, it's available, and we're lucky that it's in such free flow. If you don't like the taste, look at getting a filter; and bottled mineral water can be convenient at times too.

SODA & SUGARY DRINKS

In my house, these don't exist and are the enemy. They're a treat, and should be thought of as such. This is why I think they should only be enjoyed at special occasions (if at all, for younger children). Without question they are a fast and simple way to consume humongous amounts of empty calories— they have no nutritional value. The disastrous combination of copious amounts of sugar—often around 12 teaspoons in 2 cups—and citric acid is a nightmare for tooth decay. As people normally sip these drinks, there's no chance for the teeth to defend themselves. Over-consumption of sugar is a huge contributing factor to tooth decay in children, and multiple tooth extraction means they need to be put under general anaesthetic at a really young age. That's no joke.

FRUIT JUICE

If we drink too much, fruit juice can be equally guilty as soda and sugary drinks when it comes to tooth decay, because of the natural sugar and citric acid it contains. But consumed in the right amount, fruit juice is actually beneficial, because it also contains a lovely cocktail of vitamins, minerals, and trace elements. So, a few tricks to bear in mind: if you're buying fruit juice, only fill your glass one-quarter full, then top it up with water—this'll save you money too. At lunch and dinner time, squeeze any nice citrus and crush a little soft fruit into a pitcher, then top up with water and ice—we mix it up every day (for more inspiration go to page 254). And remember, juice doesn't have the fiber of the whole fruit, so smoothies are generally going to be more nutritious.

ALCOHOL

Here in the UK, there are more than 6,500 preventable alcohol-related deaths each year. So, bearing in mind that this book is all about optimal health, I thought a page about something that quite a lot of us enjoy, possibly too much as far as government recommendations are concerned, might be helpful.

So I want to share a few facts and some ideas and approaches I've found useful. My aim is that we can still enjoy and consume alcohol responsibly, without letting that enjoyment become detrimental to our health. I know many of you love a drink, just like I do, so let's not patronize each other, but we can always use a few good ideas, right?

LOVING OUR LIVERS

When I met liver specialists Professor Mark Thursz and Professor Gary Frost, what was fascinating to me was that the liver, our largest internal organ, which deals with alcohol and all toxins in the body, is crucial, wonderful, and extraordinary. We've only got one, so it's important not to mess it up. The liver breaks down our food and converts it into energy and essential proteins. It's centrally important in our metabolism, and in how we process nutrients and detoxify poisins. The liver also helps to remove waste products, filters toxins from the bowel, and plays a role in fighting infections.

Our livers don't like excess alcohol and excess fat—storing too much visceral fat (around our internal organs in the belly area) can increase our risk of type-2 diabetes and non-alcoholic fatty liver disease. So looking after our liver is absolutely essential, i.e., if you eat unhealthily, don't stay hydrated, and drink too much alcohol, it's not looking good. On the food front, all the recipes in this book will help keep your liver happy.

ALCOHOL ISN'T NUTRITIOUS

Regardless of quality, alcohol, as far as your body is concerned, is not nutritious and is toxic. At 7 calories per gram, it's almost up there with fat on the high-calorie scale. It can be addictive, and undoubtedly has been responsible for some of the worst behavior and decisions on the planet. So let's be responsible about it.

UK GOVERNMENT ALCOHOL RECOMMENDATIONS

+ Men: no more than 21 units a week and 3 to 4 units a day (4 units is just under 1½ pints of lager)

+ Women: no more than 14 units a week and 2 to 3 units a day (3 units is 1 large glass of wine)

So that's a shocker. My first question was: Can I save up my Monday to Thursday drinks for the weekend? And of course, government guidelines say NO! Binge drinking isn't advisable for lots of reasons, but what they do like is us having a three-day break from alcohol each week—good to know.

WHAT ARE UNITS OF ALCOHOL?

One unit is 10ml of pure alcohol. A good measure (excuse the pun) of what drinks the liver prefers is the %ABV, that's alcohol by volume. It'll be displayed on packaging as a percentage of the whole drink. The higher the percentage, the more alcohol present.

+ 1 pint of lager or cider (568ml) at 5% ABV is 2.8 units and 215 calories

+ 1 large glass of wine (250ml) at 12% ABV is 3 units and 180 calories

+ 1 shot of spirit/liqueur on ice (25ml) at 40% ABV is 1 unit and 59 calories

+ 1 gin and tonic (1 x 25ml shot and 1 x 250ml tonic) at 40% is 1 unit and 114 calories

So if calories and watching your weight is an issue, then bigging up water as your chosen drink is your biggest weapon. If you are partaking, you can see the caloric value of some of our most common drinks above.

WHAT IS A HANGOVER?

Alcohol is a diuretic, so drinking excessively can make us very dehydrated, which is why we can get a headache or feel nauseous. Crucially, alcohol consumption can disrupt and disturb our sleep. We may sleep for a longer time, but we need quality, not quantity. Excessive alcohol means we get far less deep sleep—that's why we often feel tired after drinking. Regularly hindering our sleep by drinking booze is definitely going to have a negative impact on our overall health.

HOW TO PREVENT A HANGOVER

+ Don't drink on an empty stomach—a carb-based meal can help slow the absorption of alcohol

+ Pairing alcohol intermittently with water is an easy habit to get into and very helpful

+ Two or three days off between drink-ups is much better than consecutive drinking, as it allows your liver time to recover and repair

+ It's suggested that darker spirits are more likely to give you a less clear head the next day

+ Red wines with high sulphite levels are rumored to cause headaches, but it's more likely dehydration that's the culprit—the tannins in red wine can affect some people, though

HOW TO DEAL WITH A HANGOVER

+ Keep well hydrated in the days after drinking to ensure your body rehydrates properly

+ Paracetamol can help with headaches

+ Avoid "hair of the dog" or a morning-after drink—this doesn't help, it just prolongs the pain

+ Eat a hearty breakfast—this is one situation where simple carbs can help. Or, enjoy things that will help you to rehydrate, such as soups

+ I always find a nice breath of fresh air helps, so getting outside for a little walk is advisable

+ Take a break from alcohol for a few days after a heavy session to give your liver time to recover